Advances in Contemporary Educational Thought Series
Jonas F. Soltis, Editor

The Cultural Dimensions of Educational Computing: Understanding the Non-Neutrality of Technology
C.A. BOWERS

Power and Criticism: Poststructural Investigations in Education
CLEO H. CHERRYHOLMES

The Civic Imperative: Examining the Need for Civic Education
RICHARD PRATTE

Responsive Teaching: An Ecological Approach to Classroom Patterns of Language, Culture, and Thought
C.A. BOWERS and DAVID J. FLINDERS

A Critical Theory of Education: Habermas and Our Children's Future
R.E. YOUNG

Education as a Human Right: A Theory of Curriculum and Pedagogy
DONALD VANDENBERG

Education and the Good Life: Autonomy, Altruism, and the National Curriculum
JOHN WHITE

The Challenge to Care in Schools: An Alternative Approach to Education
NEL NODDINGS

A Post-Modern Perspective on Curriculum
WILLIAM E. DOLL, JR.

Dialogue in Teaching: Theory and Practice
NICHOLAS C. BURBULES

Detachment and Concern: Essays in the Philosophy of Teaching and Teacher Education
MARGRET BUCHMANN and ROBERT E. FLODEN

The Logic of Imaginative Education: Reaching Understanding
DICK McCLEARY

Narrative Schooling: Experimental Learning and the Transformation of American Education
RICHARD L. HOPKINS

Ideology, Objectivity, and Education
JOHN WATT

Teachers' Professional Knowledge Landscapes
D. JEAN CLANDININ and F. MICHAEL CONNELLY

Teachers' Professional Knowledge Landscapes

D. JEAN CLANDININ AND F. MICHAEL CONNELLY

with

Cheryl Craig
Annie Davies
Ming Fang He
Pat Hogan
Janice Huber
Karen Whelan
Rosalie Young

Teachers College, Columbia University
New York and London

Published by Teachers College Press, 1234 Amsterdam Avenue, New York, NY 10027

Library of Congress Cataloging-in-Publication Data

Clandinin, D. Jean.
Teachers' professional knowledge landscapes / D. Jean Clandinin and F. Michael Connelly with Cheryl Craig . . . [et al.].
p. cm.—(Advances in contemporary educational thought series ; v. 15)
Includes bibliographical references and index.
ISBN 0-8077-3419-5 (cloth : acid-free paper).—ISBN 0-8077-3418-7 (paper : acid-free paper)
1. Teachers—Attitudes. 2. Teachers—Psychology. 3. Knowledge, Theory of. 4. Teaching—Psychological aspects. I. Connelly, F. Michael. II. Title. III. Series.
LB1775.C598 1995
371.1'001—dc20 94-43422

ISBN 0-8077-3418-7 (paper)
ISBN 0-8077-3419-5 (cloth)

Printed on acid-free paper

Manufactured in the United States of America

02 01 00 99 98 97 96 95 8 7 6 5 4 3 2 1

Teachers' Professional Knowledge Landscapes

D. JEAN CLANDININ AND F. MICHAEL CONNELLY

with

Cheryl Craig
Annie Davies
Ming Fang He
Pat Hogan
Janice Huber
Karen Whelan
Rosalie Young

Teachers College, Columbia University
New York and London

Published by Teachers College Press, 1234 Amsterdam Avenue, New York, NY 10027

Library of Congress Cataloging-in-Publication Data

Clandinin, D. Jean.
Teachers' professional knowledge landscapes / D. Jean Clandinin and F. Michael Connelly with Cheryl Craig . . . [et al.].
p. cm.—(Advances in contemporary educational thought series ; v. 15)
Includes bibliographical references and index.
ISBN 0-8077-3419-5 (cloth : acid-free paper).—ISBN 0-8077-3418-7 (paper : acid-free paper)
1. Teachers—Attitudes. 2. Teachers—Psychology. 3. Knowledge, Theory of. 4. Teaching—Psychological aspects. I. Connelly, F. Michael. II. Title. III. Series.
LB1775.C598 1995
371.1'001—dc20 94-43422

ISBN 0-8077-3418-7 (paper)
ISBN 0-8077-3419-5 (cloth)

Printed on acid-free paper

Manufactured in the United States of America

02 01 00 99 98 97 96 95 8 7 6 5 4 3 2 1

Contents

The conceptual framework and special language Clandinin and Connelly develop in this book open up the possibility of better understanding, of achieving a higher level of awareness, and of giving those who care deeply about the human purposes of education the wherewithal to deal creatively with the intricate problems to be found in the many-faceted landscape of education. Most important, they give teachers, teacher educators, administrators, and educational researchers a way to see into and meaningfully navigate the complex professional landscapes they live in. This book not only is a watershed in the ongoing and highly respected work of Clandinin and Connelly, it is truly an advance in contemporary educational thought and most worthy of inclusion in this series.

Jonas F. Soltis
Series Editor

Foreword

Using the metaphor of a landscape, Clandinin and Connelly and their contributing authors sketch a rich and compelling view of the epistemological and moral world in which teachers live and work. They offer new insights into the old conception of the theory-practice relation in education. They help us see teachers as moral agents as well as forced laborers in the factories of educational reformers. We see teachers both in and out of their classrooms locating themselves in different parts of a complex historical, personal, communal, and professional landscape in which moral and epistemological dilemmas abound.

The voices of teachers—preservice and experienced-in-service teachers, cooperating teachers, university teachers and researchers—all are heard in this book speaking a language Clandinin and Connelly have constructed for them to use to open up for reflection and examination the professional landscapes they journey through. There are "secret places," "sacred stories," "cover stories," the "conduit" and its "rhetoric of conclusions"—categories designed to penetrate our social construction of the reality of teaching and schooling. The formats of narrative, of storying, of plot lines, of restorying, of biographies, provide the vehicles for writing about experiences and realities, successes and failures, tensions and dilemmas, but most of all revelations and epiphanies in the lives of teachers and narrative researchers.

We follow parts of the life stories of Sonia, Benita, and Tim, who struggle to become teachers and to understand the professional landscape they are inducted into. We are also privy to a kind of reflective evaluation of the alternative teacher education program they attended. Other vignettes tell conflicting stories of teacher development and growth. We are introduced to the key idea of knowledge communities, safe havens in which genuine community provides shelter for real dialogue and the sharing of stories, human stories of relation and reflection.

In the end, Clandinin and Connelly reflect on whether theirs is a story of despair or of hopefulness. Is the professional landscape educative, miseducative, or both? Can what is revealed about teachers who doubt their power and curriculum reformers who doubt their efficacy be a means to help them see why this is happening? Can the situation be transformed for the good of all?

Acknowledgments

This book is the result of a long-term study undertaken with teachers, student teachers, and graduate students. The study would not have been possible without the collaborative support of the people with whom we worked. We especially want to acknowledge the members of the research groups at the Joint Centre for Teacher Development in Toronto, Ontario and at the Centre for Research for Teacher Education and Development in Edmonton, Alberta. In addition to the research groups our thinking has been influenced by the classes we teach and the graduate students we supervise.

We are indebted to the Social Sciences and Humanities Research Council of Canada for their financial support of the research.

Finally, we wish to thank Sherilyn Grywul and Gary Pyper for their dedicated work in entering field notes, making interview transcriptions, and preparing this manuscript. They mastered the mysteries of sending formatted text files back and forth across the country.

PART I

PROFESSIONAL KNOWLEDGE LANDSCAPES

CHAPTER 1

Teachers' Professional Knowledge Landscapes: Secret, Sacred, and Cover Stories

F. Michael Connelly and D. Jean Clandinin

We want to ask the question of how the embodied, narrative, relational knowledge teachers carry autobiographically and by virtue of their formal education shapes, and is shaped by, their professional knowledge context. This question has been in the background of our work for many years. Beginning with our early studies, where we concentrated on teachers' personal practical knowledge, we understood the intellectual risk of the work, which might, for some, encourage too partial a view of teachers' knowledge. We were constantly reminded that teachers do not work in isolation, nor do they work in environments solely of their own choosing. For example, given our interest at that time in a local board of education's race-relations policy, a senior administrator of the district in which Bay Street is situated advised us to work in Bay Street School. His reason was supplied via a metaphor of the funnel, which, he claimed, board officials used to pour different policies into different schools. No school, he said, could cope with all of the board's policies at once. The funneling process allowed the administration to selectively target schools for specific board policies and Bay Street was targeted for the race-relations policy. Consequently, most of the teachers with whom we worked in Bay Street did not choose to work in the context of that policy. It was given to them.

The metaphor of the funnel inspired us to think about how school policies were fed into schools. However, we put this matter on the back burner because our interest was in trying to understand how teachers knew the board's race-relations policy and, more generally, how we could give an account of teacher knowledge. At that time we were not interested in the "funneling" process. We were, however, aware that what was funneled into schools made a difference to teachers. Furthermore, we were aware that it was not only a question of what was funneled in, but also a matter of how school participants professionalized policy material pouring forth from the funnel, thereby making policy part of the communal knowledge environment for teachers in the targeted schools. This metaphor haunted us while we pursued the study of teachers' individual experiences. Now we want to pay attention to what is funneled in and its consequences for teacher knowledge.

This book is our attempt to sketch out our thinking. The outlines of our argument are as follows: When we turned to the literature of professional knowledge we found it to be large and diverse. A number of literature strands appear to be at work: teachers' professional development in the culture of schools (Lieberman, 1988; Lieberman & Miller, 1992); improvement of learning by the improvement of teaching via more professionally knowledgeable teachers (Darling-Hammond & Wise, 1992; Reynolds, 1989); the enhancement of the status of the profession (Barringer, 1993); the professional knowledge base of teachers (Shulman & Sykes, 1986; Tom & Valli, 1990); knowledge utilization by teachers (Fullan, 1991; Huberman, 1983); and other strands. For the most part, these literature strands are not heavily cross-referenced, nor integrated in any serious way. We were uncertain about how to bring the literature together in a way that would help us deal with the question of how to contextualize teachers' personal practical knowledge. We decided we needed to generate a set of terms for our own purposes. The metaphor of the funnel was always provocative in our thinking and led us, since it is essentially a theory-practice construct, to frame our thinking in theory-practice terms. In this book we elaborate a metaphor of a professional knowledge landscape that we imagine to be positioned at the interface of theory and practice in teachers' lives. We try to show that the professional knowledge landscape that teachers inhabit creates epistemological dilemmas that we understand narratively in terms of secret, sacred, and cover stories. The metaphor of the professional knowledge landscape provides a way to contextualize research-based understandings of teachers' personal practical knowledge.

THE PROFESSIONAL KNOWLEDGE LANDSCAPE

A landscape metaphor is particularly well suited to our purpose. It allows us to talk about space, place, and time. Furthermore, it has a sense of expansiveness and the possibility of being filled with diverse people, things, and events in different relationships. Understanding professional knowledge as comprising a landscape calls for a notion of professional knowledge as composed of a wide variety of components and influenced by a wide variety of people, places, and things. Because we see the professional knowledge landscape as composed of relationships among people, places, and things, we see it as both an intellectual and a moral landscape.

In our work we noticed the intensity with which teachers spoke of feeling disturbed by their experiences of the landscape. They said that it was not mainly their work with students that disturbed them. It was something else, something they could not quite name. As we thought about this we realized the obvious—namely, that teachers spend part of their time in classrooms and part of their time in other professional, communal places. Teachers and classrooms are so intricately linked in the professional literature that it is easy to forget that teachers spend many hours each week outside of the classroom with people other than students. The focus of our interest on personal practical knowledge studies had been on teachers in their classrooms. In order to understand what disturbed teachers about their professional lives, we discovered that we needed to understand the relationship between how teachers live in their classrooms and how teachers live in those other professional, communal places. These are two fundamentally different places on the landscape, the one behind the classroom door with students, and the other in professional places with others. We believe, and will try to make the case here, that this split existence is central to the disturbance teachers feel. As we reflected on teachers' lives in these two places on the landscape, we remarked on the dilemma-laden quality of being in both. Lampert (1985), Lyons (1990), and others, have drawn attention to teacher dilemmas within the classroom while Cuban (1992) has drawn attention to teachers' out-of-classroom professional dilemmas. We want to think about the dilemmas created by moving in and out of the classroom on the professional knowledge landscape. We want to describe the uneasy state of teachers' professional lives as part and parcel of moral and epistemological dilemmas associated with living in, and repeatedly crossing back and forth between, two epistemologically different places on the landscape.

EPISTEMOLOGICAL DILEMMAS

The best known epistemological dilemmas in education are defined by the terms *theory* and *practice*. In this section we unpack a notion of theory and practice. We do so because, though this is well-trodden territory, the discussion in the literature inevitably focuses on the relations of theory and practice as they occur on the landscape. But our take on the notions of theory and practice draws attention to the epistemological quality of what is funneled into the landscape, as well as to the funnel itself. These considerations are central to the epistemological dilemmas we wish to describe for teachers on the landscape.

Educators of all persuasions, and wherever situated on an imagined continuum joining theoretical and practical activities, are enjoined to be, at one and the same time, theoretical and practical. At one end of the imagined continuum, educational researchers and theorists are expected to produce practically useful theoretical knowledge. But the record is bleak. The kind of research and theory produced tends to be held in little theoretical regard by disciplinary scholars and held to be of little practical value by practitioners. Education researchers who opt for more local, practical work tend to be dismissed by their own scholarly academy, while gaining little by way of practical acceptance. And researchers who opt for more theoretical pursuits tend to disappear from notice in the practical world while gaining little by way of status with their disciplinary colleagues. Writers from different points on the academic spectrum have discussed this general matter (Clifford & Guthrie, 1988; Cuban, 1988; Goodlad, 1990; Lanier & Little, 1986; Sinclair & Harrison, 1988).

At the other end of the imagined continuum, teacher practitioners are expected not merely to teach in a way that embodies an expert practical knowledge of teaching but to do so reflectively. Furthermore, teaching, the practical knowledge it exhibits, and reflecting on it are thought to be dangerously narcissistic unless teachers use theoretical knowledge about teaching, learning, and subject matter taught to them by theoreticians and their representatives. When teachers make an effort to use this theoretical knowledge as intended, they are often thought to be unprofessional, with insufficient confidence in their practical experience to work out what action should be taken. And when, as is more commonly the case, they make it practical by personalizing theoretical knowledge for their work, they are frequently thought to be intellectually conservative and resistant to positive change.

The described situations are dilemmas because neither researchers in their situation nor teachers in theirs can have it both ways theoretically and practically. "Dilemmas," says Cuban (1992), "are conflict-filled situations that require choices because competing, highly prized values cannot be fully satisfied" (p. 6). Cuban also says that dilemmas are not soluble, something educators at all levels experience relative to theory and practice. As educators, therefore, we work in an uneasy professional environment never sure of our position relative to theory and practice, constantly confronted by the conflicting claims of theory and practice.

Perhaps because the terms *theory* and *practice,* and the epistemological dilemmas they create, persist and will not go away, the terms have become overly familiar in educational discourse. They are used so lightly in such statements as "There is nothing so practical as good theory" that it is easy to lose sight of the fundamental distinction between theoretical knowledge and practical knowledge. The difference between the two cannot easily be overcome by urging academics to be more practical and urging practitioners to value and make better use of theory. In our view, the smoothing and glossing over of the distinction has been harmful to working through fundamental problems of school reform, teacher education, and the nature of teachers' professionalism.

So far we have made the case that the terms *theory* and *practice* create dilemmas in the lives of professional educators. Before directly pursuing our question on teachers' professional knowledge landscapes, we need to unpack the relationship of practical knowledge to practice and theoretical knowledge to theory and to say more about the epistemological quality of this set of considerations. We are clearer, at least in our own minds, about the relationship between teachers' personal practical knowledge and their practice because that relationship is part and parcel of our studies of teachers' knowledge. What we mean by teachers' knowledge is that body of convictions and meanings, conscious or unconscious, that have arisen from experience (intimate, social, and traditional) and that are expressed in a person's practices. We use the term *expression* to refer to a quality of knowledge rather than to its more common usage as an application or translation of knowledge. It is a kind of knowledge that has arisen from circumstances, practices, and undergoings that themselves had affective content for the person in question. Therefore, practice is part of what we mean by personal practical knowledge. Indeed, practice, broadly conceived to include intellectual acts and self-exploration, is all we have to go on. When we see practice, we see personal practical knowledge at work.

Turning to the relationship of theory to theoretical knowledge, it is worth noting that popular usage more or less reduces the two terms to the same meaning. When people use the word *theory,* they tend to mean the codified knowledge found in books. Without entering into a full discussion of the issues at work, we want to point out that this collapsing of the terms strips theoretical knowledge of the inquiry that gave rise to it. Following this, a more complete account of the meaning of theoretical knowledge would include, in addition to the codified outcomes of inquiry, an understanding of the phenomena represented, the inquiry methodologies at work, the inquiry context, and the role of human agency in the inquiry. Thus, when the terms *theory* and *theoretical knowledge* are collapsed to mean the codified outcomes of inquiry, most of what makes that knowledge meaningful and understandable is lost. Schwab (1962) called these stripped-down knowledge claims a "rhetoric of conclusions." Much the same can be said for policy, which is usually taken to mean government, board of education, or other statements stripped of the public deliberative process that gave rise to them (Reid, 1987). Policy stripped of its deliberative origins has the abstract epistemological quality of theoretical knowledge stripped of its inquiry origins. Policy, therefore, also has the quality of a rhetoric of conclusions.

It is important to our argument to mark out the epistemological dilemmas created by the distinction between theory and practice and to characterize what passes for theory and policy relative to the funnel. What we have so far said in this section is that the theoretical knowledge and policy directives that pass for theory and are fed into the landscape via the funnel are, for the most part, epistemologically inadequate. There are serious consequences for teachers' professional knowledge flowing from these considerations. We describe these in the section "The Professional Knowledge Landscape Outside the Classroom." We now turn our attention to the funnel.

THEORY-PRACTICE RELATIONS: THE FUNNEL AS A SACRED STORY

North American education is so deeply embedded with a notion of theory-driven practice that it is difficult to get a hearing for an alternative view. The school administrator's metaphor of the funnel aptly expresses the relationship. The universality and taken-for-grantedness of the supremacy of theory over practice gives it the quality of a sacred story (Crites, 1971). Crites makes the point that sacred stories are so pervasive they remain mostly unnoticed and when named are hard to define: "These stories seem to be elusive expressions of stories that cannot be fully and directly told, because they live, so to speak, in the arms and legs and bellies of the celebrants. These stories lie too deep in the consciousness of the people to be directly told" (p. 294). The relationship of theory to practice has this quality and for that reason we say that the professional knowledge landscape for teachers is embedded in a sacred story. This is also the reason why it is necessary to use metaphors such as the funnel to talk about the relationship. In a review of the curriculum development and implementation literature we (Clandinin & Connelly, 1992) drew on Reddy's (1979) linguistic work and Johnson's (1987, 1989) philosophic work to speak of the relationship as a conduit.

Reddy (1979) argued that "the stories English speakers tell about communication are largely determined by semantic structures of the language itself" (p. 285). The dominant "communication structure" for Reddy is the conduit metaphor, which Johnson (1987) summarizes:

1. Ideas and thoughts are objects.
2. Words and sentences are containers for these objects.
3. Communication consists in finding the right word—container for your idea-object, sending this filled container along the conduit or through space to the hearer, who must take the idea-object out of the word-container.

The conduit is a metaphor that allows us to name the sacred story and to give a sense of how it functions in relating theory and practice in education. Specifically, the conduit allows us to imagine how the sacred story shapes teachers' professional knowledge landscapes. In broad outline, here is how it works.

In his series of articles on the practical, Schwab (1970, 1971, 1973, 1983) described a methodology, which he called the "eclectic," for readying theoretical knowledge for practice. Schwab's point was that there was too much theoretical knowledge, and in the wrong form, for practical use without translation via a readying process in which theoretical knowledge was made practical. What Schwab drew attention to is standard practice in curriculum studies and teacher education and comes under such headings as "selecting, organizing, and presenting" ideas and materials (e.g., Tyler, 1950). Schwab, of course, had a specific methodology in mind, which would retain the inquiry basis of knowledge. However, what we see happening is that the readying process, in which theoretical knowledge is most always interpreted to be the codified outcomes of inquiry, strips knowledge claims of their inquiry origins.

Schwab's name for this stripped down theoretical knowledge was "a rhetoric of conclusions": theoretical knowledge claims uprooted from their origins and standing in abstract, objective independence. This "theoretical" knowledge is then packaged for teachers in textbooks, curriculum materials, and professional-development workshops. In effect, the readying and packaging of theoretical knowledge in education closely fits the conduit metaphor described above. For the most part a rhetoric of conclusions is packaged and transmitted via the conduit to the teachers' professional knowledge landscape.

We do not wish to imply that the only kind of theoretical knowledge in the conduit is a rhetoric of conclusions. Sometimes, for instance, research articles and narratives of inquiry, two of Schwab's hopes for the eclectic, are fed into the landscape via the conduit. But a big part of what is fed through the conduit is a rhetoric of conclusions.

THE PROFESSIONAL KNOWLEDGE LANDSCAPE OUTSIDE THE CLASSROOM

We are now in a position to give an epistemological characterization of the professional knowledge landscape outside the classroom. At a surface level, this place on the landscape consists of teachers' personal practical knowledge, ideas, curriculum programs, administrative structures, policies, and lists of teachers' certifiable knowledge, skills, and attitudes. At this point we need to follow through on the consequences of the conduit for this part of the landscape.

Teachers are required to know, understand, discuss, and do something with the knowledge poured into the landscape via the conduit. This knowledge is packaged in textbooks, pamphlets, workshops, staff meetings, information sessions, memos, and the like. Theoretically it appears as a rhetoric of conclusions and as such it is neither theoretical nor practical. Likewise, the language that teachers, administrators, and others use to discuss these conduit-delivered materials is a language that is neither theoretical nor practical. Thus, the material in the landscape and the language used to discuss it are neither theoretical nor practical, though they have features of both. Rather, the material and the language are abstract. Abstract diagrams, assessment plans, factors, school improvement plans, schemata, forces, research conclusions, research prescriptions, policy prescriptions, and so forth, fill the landscape. Teachers, consultants, administrators, and others discuss and give their own accounts of these research findings and policy directions. In this discussion and accounting process, the language becomes increasingly abstract as individuals try to make sense of already very abstract material. This place on the professional knowledge landscape, insofar as it is due to the conduit connecting practice and theory, is a landscape of abstractions.

We see this place on the landscape as abstract in two senses. In the first sense of abstraction we mean it is not grounded. There are few, if any, links between the abstract statements of policy and research coming from the conduit and the phenomenological world to which they refer. There are no people, events, or things—only words cut off from their origins. Life and what we might call the existential world are not involved. The situation is reminiscent of MacIntyre's (1981) observation that much of moral theory has become theoretically abstract and is a discourse of words without human presence. In this first sense of abstraction, this place on the professional knowledge landscape seems to float untethered. And as more material is delivered into the conduit by a worried public, and as more abstract professional development talk occurs to ensure that teachers get it right for the sake of school improvement, the more airborne becomes the landscape.

The professional knowledge landscape outside the classroom is abstract in another sense. The research conclusions, the policy prescriptions, and so on are torn out of their historical, narrative contexts. This strips away the historical meaning that situates the knowledge claims in the conditions and context of inquiry and in the subjectivity associated with human presence in inquiry. Packaged knowledge and policy claims from the conduit have an ethereal quality, as if they somehow appeared and exist independent of human agency and the conditions of inquiry. In this second sense of abstraction, this place on the landscape, insofar as it is a landscape influenced by the conduit, has an unconditional and depersonalized quality.

Teachers are expected to know the abstract rhetoric of conclusions without even the statistical qualifiers that mark the most elementary research methods training. And teachers are not, by and large, expected to personalize conduit materials by considering how materials fit their personality and teaching styles, classrooms, students, and so forth. In general, then, teachers are screened from the subjectivity of human agency that gave rise to the material in inquiry and in policy deliberation while being taught that their own agency with regard to the decontextualized and denarrativized material would amount to incompetence or disobedience.

A further epistemological consequence of this sense of abstraction is that there is no entry point for debate and discussion of the funneled materials. They, necessarily, must be taken as givens. To debate their appropriateness is to question someone's authority. Discussion, such as it is, is removed from matters of substance to matters of personality and power.

The sacred story of the conduit relationship of theory and practice imposes yet another critical feature on the landscape. The professional knowledge landscape is a moral one. Material enters the landscape from the conduit with a moral orientation. Nothing enters the landscape value-neutral; nothing is there for interest's sake to be discussed and understood as such. Everything comes with a moral push with which teachers are expected to do something.

This moral orientation and sense of persuasion are due to the sacred story, which requires that the descriptive "is" of theoretical knowledge be transformed into a prescriptive "ought" in practice. The conduit is prescriptive; it is a conduit of shoulds. Thus, what is dripped down the conduit is a moral, abstract rhetoric of conclusions. Indeed, the professional knowledge landscape is so filled with various moral admonitions, many of them conflicting one with another, that educational administrators and policymakers higher up the conduit often find it necessary to formulate vision statements in attempts to give moral shape to the professional knowledge landscapes of schools and school districts. Visions give the landscape a degree of moral unity where conflicting moral goods, and personal interpretations of what is right, can be shaped and judged. Taylor's (1989) *Sources of the Self* gives a philosophical account of what it means to live in a moral landscape oriented to moral horizons that establish moral boundaries. What is special, perhaps peculiar, about the out-of-classroom place on the moral landscape is the degree to which the moral orientation and horizons are set by others pouring moral material into the landscape via the theory-practice conduit.

THE PROFESSIONAL KNOWLEDGE LANDSCAPE IN THE CLASSROOM: A SAFE PLACE FOR SECRET STORIES

Classrooms are a special place within the professional knowledge landscape. Those of us who work in conceptualizing teacher knowledge have focused on teachers as they work in classrooms. Classrooms are, in Schwab's (1970, 1971, 1973) terms, practical places. They are places of action where teachers teach and where curriculum is made, at least the curriculum that matters as far as students are concerned. Earlier we noted that the practices of teaching and curriculum making were expressions of teachers' knowledge. For an excellent epistemological review of teachers' knowledge research, see Fenstermacher (1994).

Our best understanding of teacher knowledge is a narrative one (Carter, 1993; Clandinin, 1986; Connelly & Clandinin, 1990; Elbaz, 1983). In this view of teachers' knowledge, teachers know their lives in terms of stories. They live stories, tell stories of those lives, retell stories with changed possibilities, and relive the changed stories. In this narrative view of teachers' knowledge, we mean more than teachers' telling stories of specific children and events. We mean that their way of being in the classroom is storied: As teachers they are characters in their own stories of teaching, which they author.

We want to point out how dramatically different narrative knowledge in practice is both from theoretical knowledge and from the abstract rhetoric of conclusions found in the professional knowledge landscape outside the classroom. Narrative knowledge, theoretical knowledge, and an abstract rhetoric of conclusions are epistemologically and morally different from one another.

Important to our argument is another characteristic of the professional knowledge landscape in classrooms that is seen clearly by comparison with the professional knowledge landscape outside classrooms. One of the commonplaces of thinking about the classroom is that it is a private place in the sense that teachers and students work behind a closed door.

The sense of the closed door is so prominent that efforts to bring parents into the classrooms and to have cross-visitations among teachers, visits from the principal, and so forth, are thought to be somewhat daring and breaking with tradition. There is a sense of autonomy about teachers in their classrooms, a sense of ownership ("This is my classroom"). So much is the teachers' autonomy behind the classroom door in evidence that some have said that this is the "problem" of professionalism (Darling-Hammond & Wise, 1992).

The privacy of the classroom plays an important epistemological function. It is a safe place, generally free from scrutiny, where teachers are free to live stories of practice. These lived stories are essentially secret ones. Furthermore, when these secret lived stories are told, they are, for the most part, told only to other teachers in still other secret places. The staff room comes to mind, although this is increasingly not a safe place for the telling of these stories. Safe for the telling are special times and places such as Friday afternoon gatherings out of school.

Some might object to this line of thought, recognizing that students are active storytellers about classrooms. However, with the exception of dramatic stories, retold by parents, student stories tend not to enter the professional knowledge landscape.

In our focus on understanding the classroom as a safe place for the living of secret practical stories, we do not wish to glorify secrecy. We do think that part of the power of the teaching act comes in its secrecy. But, at the same time, the secrecy of the teaching act also opens it to abuse. Being in a secret place without reflection brought on by professional discussions with others may lead to an inward-looking personal cultivation. There are endless examples of racist, sexist practices carried on in secrecy and we, along with those who call for the professionalization of teaching, are concerned about this. Nevertheless, we do not want to lose sight of the fact that in the end teaching is a secret enterprise and depends for its success on the maintenance of a safe place for those secret acts of teaching to occur.

What is missing in the classroom is a place for teachers to tell and retell their stories of teaching. The classroom can become a place of endless, repetitive, living out of stories without possibility for awakenings and transformations. Schön (1991) and others (e.g., Russell & Munby, 1992) argue that there is reflection-in-action. They believe that this process contributes to "knowing-in-action." We do not want to discount this possibility but we do think that the possibilities for reflective awakenings and transformations are limited when one is alone. Teachers need others in order to engage in conversations where stories can be told, reflected back, heard in different ways, retold, and relived in new ways in the safety and secrecy of the classroom.

These conversations, by and large, have to take place outside of the classroom. When teachers leave their classrooms and move into another place on the professional knowledge landscape, they leave the safe secrecy of the classroom and enter a public place on the landscape. Walking out of the classroom is walking into a dramatically different epistemological and moral place on the landscape. By and large, as we will argue, this place is also not an hospitable place for telling teaching stories.

CROSSING THE BOUNDARY: CREATING THE DILEMMAS

The language of the conduit permeates the out-of-classroom landscape. This is not a language of story, it is a language of abstraction. The language of abstraction, a rhetoric of conclusions, is propositional, relational among concepts, impersonal, situation-independent, objective, nontemporal, ahistorical, and generic. In contrast, teachers leave behind the classroom language of story, which is prototypical, relational among people, personal, contextual, subjective, temporal, historical, and specific. Furthermore, the out-of-classroom landscape's abstract language is morally laden. Nothing comes through the conduit as merely theoretical knowledge to be known and understood: it always comes as an implied prescription for teachers' actions. Teachers' narrative classroom knowledge is also moral but it is a morality that adheres to the teachers' self-authoring of classroom stories. Thus, as teachers cross the boundary between a safe place for living the secret stories of teaching to a place of moral persuasion and of abstract knowledge, they move across a boundary separating markedly different epistemological and moral parts of the landscape. Returning to the classroom from a staff meeting on a new board of education curriculum plan, for instance, is a move from a place of abstractions and propositional reasoning to a place where the prototypical life unfolds.

The boundary, of course, is semipermeable. Teachers carry their narrative knowledge with them outside the classroom and the rhetoric of conclusions invades the classroom at every turn. This semipermeability creates epistemological and moral dilemmas because teachers cannot have it both ways. They cannot simultaneously live and talk a concrete narrative knowledge and an abstract rhetoric of conclusions. Crossing back and forth between the two parts of the professional knowledge landscape creates epistemological and moral dilemmas for teachers.

In the out-of-classroom part of the professional knowledge landscape, teachers and others speak the language of the conduit, that is, they speak of plans, of results, and of policy implications. However, the language of the conduit is not a language that allows teachers to tell of what matters most to them, that is, stories of children and classroom events. Teachers experience this as a dilemma. If they tell stories of the secret events of the classroom as expressions of their knowledge, they are portrayed as uncertain, tentative, nonexpert characters. If teachers were, as the romantics claim, autonomous this would not be a problem. But teachers are accountable to others on the landscape and to still others positioned along the conduit. On the other hand, if they respond to this accountability by talking about unit plans, lesson plans, evaluation, goals, and strategies, they are portrayed as certain, expert professionals. But this abstract talk, disconnected from their teaching situations, is mostly irrelevant to their practical concerns.

How do teachers manage this dilemma? Increasingly, teachers tell us they live and tell cover stories in the out-of-classroom professional knowledge landscape, stories in which they portray themselves as characters who are certain, expert people. These cover stories are a way of managing their dilemma. The tensions in managing their dilemma in this way is what we first noticed in teachers' feelings of being disturbed on the landscape. This book tells stories of teachers' professional lives and explores the significance of the stories for understanding teachers' professional knowledge.

CHAPTER 2

Dilemmas in Crossing the Boundaries on the Professional Knowledge Landscape

Cheryl Craig

As a teacher, I live in two different professional places. One is the relational world inside the classroom where I co-construct meaning with my students. The other is the abstract world where I live with everyone outside my classroom, a world where I meet all the other aspects of the educational enterprise such as the philosophies, the techniques, the materials, and the expectations that I will enact certain educational practices. While each of these places is distinctive, neither is totally self-contained. Together these places form the professional knowledge landscape that frames my work as an educator.

Frequently, events such as the ones I will describe occur concurrently in these two different places and I am called to respond to them. The following two episodes—the transfer of Carla, an underprivileged student, from my classroom and my attendance at a school system testing meeting—happened in two different places on my professional knowledge landscape. Each of these episodes held meaning for me and below I illustrate how each created dilemmas (Lyons, 1990) in my knowing. I will argue that the tensions in my knowing arose from the ways my moral horizons were lodged in the professional knowledge landscape. I begin by sharing the two episodes.

THE FIRST EPISODE: CARLA

At the beginning of the school year, Carla and I were both new to the school. Carla was an attractive girl with long, curly hair, a cherubic face, and shiny blue eyes. She was small for her eight years of age.

Carla was in third grade but her development was more like that of a first-grader. She had two sisters in the school, a biological sister in grade

2 whom I saw as being full of anger and a half-sister in grade 1 who was a fetal alcohol syndrome (FAS) child. Carla, her two school-age sisters, and an infant sister lived in a rental unit at the edge of the community with her mother, her mother's boyfriend, and her biological father, who remained with the family as a boarder.

My story became interwoven with Carla's when we were both newcomers to a small school in a middle-class neighborhood in a western Canadian city. The school had a long tradition of offering quality education. A story often told about the school was that it was like a private school in a public school system. Because of its reputation, many affluent, out-of-boundary parents enrolled their children there.

Carla's socioeconomic and family circumstances contrasted with that of most of the other students. Some days she and her sisters came to school wearing inadequate clothing—for example, they might appear at school wearing no socks and torn canvas shoes in subzero weather. On other days the girls' lunches were inadequate. As I conversed with Carla, trying to understand her situation, I learned that she made her sisters' lunches and helped them get dressed for school. No wonder Carla came to school exhausted. She was drained from dealing with one sister's anger, another sister's lack of focus, and another sister's infant needs. Carla was expected to act, and was acting, as a parent.

In the eight months I worked with Carla, her life stories, which shaped her school story, became apparent. And these stories served to silence my frustration with Carla's careless work and her frequent socializing in the classroom. When I placed her school story in her life-story frame, I came to see that school was the only place where she could be a child. It was the only place where Carla was free from adult responsibilities.

But school could be a difficult place for Carla. When other students discussed experiences of holidaying in California, Florida, and abroad, Carla could not respond. She could only name places she wished to visit: the zoo, a movie theater, a library, all common places within the city limits. And while other students shared show-and-tell items of commercial value, Carla shared scraps of nothingness: labels from common food products, discarded trinkets she found in the garbage, and bleak stories from her own experience. Carla's Writers' Workshop stories revealed even more of her lived story. She wrote numerous pieces about "the monster" in her house, featuring her mother's boyfriend as the main character. She also wrote compelling stories in which she imagined a better life for herself: a life in which she and her sisters would live in a stable family situation and own a house and a car, commonplace possessions of the other students in the class. And I encouraged Carla to write these pieces. I wanted her to explore ways she could retell her life. I wanted Carla to experience the power of writing to learn.

While I have previously taught less privileged students, none have touched me so profoundly as Carla. In my past experience, there was always a group of students in situations like Carla's. They supported one another. Accordingly, these students did not have to rub shoulders with students of more affluent parents as did Carla.

Having Carla and her sisters in the school evoked a variety of responses from both students and parents. At first, some students giggled at, or were embarrassed by, Carla's stories and her show-and-tell items. Some corrected her spoken English; others spoke of her poor eating habits in the lunchroom. Meanwhile, some parents claimed that the family did not belong in the school. They argued that she and her sisters were taking up too much teacher time. Other parents were ambivalent about the situation while still others expressed support of Carla, her sisters, and the teachers who educated them.

As time passed, however, there were acts of compassion toward Carla and her sisters. I particularly remember one mother bringing Halloween costumes to school for Carla and her sisters because she knew they would not have them. And for one day in her life, Carla was transformed into a dazzling princess. Another girl told her parents about Carla's shabby winter coat and Carla was soon outfitted with sporty skiwear. A boy gave Carla a set of pencil crayons. Still other children slipped money into Carla's hand on special days like Book or Doughnut Day, having asked their parents for extra money for Carla or cutting back on their own purchases. Carla's situation also touched my own 14-year-old son. Jeff often came to the classroom to listen to her read and to edit her work. Our school staff responded as well. We adopted the family as a secret Christmas project and donated food and other gifts.

One day shortly after Christmas, Carla came to school particularly troubled. She announced that her mother was going to put her FAS sister up for adoption. Everyone in the school was horrified. This was a story clearly outside the margins of the acceptable stories students shared at this school. As the week unfolded, it became apparent the family situation had deteriorated. She told stories about the boyfriend's being charged with theft and stories of vicious arguments between her mother and her boyfriend. One day Carla was even more upset. The boyfriend had left, taking with him the Nintendo, a Christmas gift a teacher from a previous school had given them. Carla was angry that he had stolen one of their toys, but even more frightened for her family's safety. Carla said her family would be moving immediately.

After Carla's announcement, the other students in the class and I organized a surprise party for her. This was something I had never done before in my career. Never before had I singled out one student to honor. We worked hard to make the party like the birthday parties we knew Carla did not have.

The next day, Carla's mother came to get her and her sisters with the baby and a new boyfriend. Carla's mother said she, her daughters, her new boyfriend, and her ex-husband had found an apartment on the other side of the city.

As Carla, her sisters, her mother, and the new boyfriend loaded into a late-model car, we teachers tearfully waved goodbye from the front entrance of the school. Each of us had cared deeply for Carla and her sisters and tried to address the harsh realities that presented themselves in our classroom contexts. We also used the occasion to reflect on the girls' academic growth. Carla and her sisters would still not be considered "average" students in our school but they had shown considerable growth. We imagined what their possibilities might have been if our stories were intertwined for a longer period of time. But most of all, we discussed what Carla, her sisters, and their situation taught the other students, their parents, and ourselves about life. We considered the hollowness of some school system goals, the testing goal in particular. I can remember turning to my colleagues and saying ironically: "Our school scores will look so much better now that they are gone. If having high test scores in our school is what education is all about, I wonder why we all are feeling so crummy?"

INTERLUDE

The next day as I raced out of my classroom to attend a school system testing meeting, the teacher across the hall flagged me down. "Mrs. Craig, why have your students moved a miniature desk into my grade 5–6 classroom? Do you think I have someone small enough to fit it?" I gaped at her. I knew whose desk she was talking about. It was Carla's desk. But my understanding was that my colleague had requested it for use as a learning center. And on her request, three students from my class had moved it across the hall. Now it was my colleague's turn to gape. Clearly, she and I had different versions of a story. Together we grappled to figure out the situation. Then it came to us. Two of the boys who moved the desk had sat in the group with Carla. The sight of her empty desk must have disturbed them. By coincidence, they were also the boys who cleaned my colleague's room. This provided them with a perfect foil for inventing the story they told me. The other teacher did not need the desk but my students needed to get rid of it. The desk was an uncomfortable reminder of Carla.

THE SECOND EPISODE: THE SCHOOL SYSTEM TESTING MEETING

I arrived late at the testing meeting. I missed the coffee, doughnuts, and platitudes. The serious presentation had begun.

We were told that our school jurisdiction was not taking the provincial achievement testing program as seriously as we should and that our collective attitude toward achievement testing was somewhat cavalier. Our public was dissatisfied with education and we needed to be more accountable to them. The public saw achievement tests as the way to measure our educational successes. And we needed to produce those scores to be accountable to our public and to win their support. We were then informed that the trustees of our school jurisdiction had requested that school test scores be made available to the public. The trustees wanted scores to be released to newspapers showing which schools were below, at, or above school system and provincial means. These school scores were also to be published in school newsletters and made available to parents. Never before had we publicly documented test scores in our school system, although parents had always had access to their children's scores.

As I sat back, numbed by these mandates, I reflected on the many things that disturbed me about the testing program. I thought about how I had come to view knowledge as the personal and social construction/reconstruction of meaning and how my view conflicted with the technical-rational view of knowledge inherent in the tests. I thought about how disconnected the tests were from students' life experiences and how strange the format was for grade-3 students. I also thought about how I and other teachers who worked daily with students had been left out of this evaluation process.

My reflections then shifted to our school system. I noted how the present mandates conflicted with their past policy and goal statements. I marveled at how quickly the system story had changed under public pressure. And the word *politics* reverberated in my head: the politics of what counts as knowledge; the politics of who decides how knowing will be represented; the politics of who knowers are in the school system; the politics of who tells whom what matters in the school system.

Then inequities danced across my mind. I wondered how useful it would be to identify below-average schools. Surely we all knew schools with low scores just as we knew schools with high scores. But what could testing do for schools? It is inevitable that there will always be schools below average and others above.

I left my reflections when I heard the speaker bringing the meeting to closure. I glanced at my teacher colleagues. It was obvious we were all struggling to make sense of what we had just heard.

THE DILEMMAS

Each of these episodes from my storied life as a teacher created dilemmas in my knowing (Lyons, 1990)—dilemmas for which I found no easy solutions.

In the Carla episode, I recognized a tension between the school story and the life story Carla brought to the school. This tension was made explicit by some parents. Even before I knew Carla as a student, I knew that her situation in the school context was being monitored. I also knew that the parent group had scrutinized particular students and staff members in the past. Attempting to remove people who were seen as being on the edges was almost an annual event.

I realized that Carla did not fit the school story. She rushed through her work and often socialized with her peers. As I learned Carla's life story, I appreciated her desire for more conversational spaces. I purposely built these spaces into her classroom activities. I was what Marland (1977) calls "stategically lenient" with Carla.

But this created a dilemma. In my efforts to respond to Carla's situation, I created a situation that might lead to her removal. The physical space of my classroom was often on public view. Furthermore, I had parent volunteers working daily with me. I did not want anyone gathering classroom evidence to support the argument that Carla's family did not fit in the school.

What could I do? An answer came through my son, Jeff. He came to the classroom to help my students edit their writing. Jeff realized that Carla needed special attention. As he worked with her, she started to gain confidence. As Jeff helped Carla develop her sense of agency, he too experienced a sense of agency. This kept him coming back to help her and kept him inquiring as to her progress.

Rather than my creating a cover story of Carla for the parents by acting as if she were no different from my other students, I decided to have her work with parent volunteers just as she had with Jeff. In these encounters with parents, something happened. Rather than seeing Carla and her sisters as marks to be wiped off the slate, some parents began to explore other ways of telling Carla's story. This happened at the same time their children and I were exploring ways we could be a more caring and responsive classroom community. Furthermore, as some children and their parents reported, this caring attitude spilled over to the homes.

THE TESTING MEETING DILEMMA

In the testing meeting episode, I also faced a dilemma. This dilemma was set up for me by the information delivered via the conduit. While I disagreed with the premises on which the testing program was based, I had no choice as to whether my students would write the tests. All my grade-3 students would be writing the examinations and by school system mandate, the school test scores would be published. As with everything funneled down the conduit, I could not debate its appropriateness, for to do so was to question someone's authority. The only choice I had was in how I would prepare my students. Would I turn story writing into a mechanistic science so my students would excel in the tests? Would I fill their heads with rules of thumb to beat the testing system, such things as: "Think of unusual titles"; "Include conversation in your story"; "Make lots of revisions to your first draft"; "Even if you don't know the answer shade in a box"—all of which would guarantee them higher marks according to the available standardized marking system? These out-of-context suggestions were contrary to the way I teach. But the way I teach might lead to lower test results. What was in the best interests of my students?

MY MORAL HORIZONS

So far, I have described two episodes and the dilemmas created by them. In this section, I use the episodes to explore my moral experiences in two different places on the professional knowledge landscape.

First, I turn to the Carla episode. In that episode, the professional knowledge landscape is shaped by a school story of high academic achievement. This story framed many parents' moral horizons and was expressed in school and school system mission statements. Teachers were expected to live it out. I experienced these expectations on the out-of-classroom landscape and lived them out in my classroom.

I recognized that Carla did not fit the school story. My dilemma was how to adjust my practices to include her and still remain within the range of acceptable stories in the school. I became more tolerant of Carla's behavior and I set the tone for other students being tolerant of her. I created situations in which my students and their parents met Carla face-to-face and responded to her as a person, not as an out-of-place aberration in a school story of achievement. And in these "commonplaces of human experience" (Lane, 1988), they also adapted their moral horizons to include Carla. In spite of the many things I could not change in my telling of the Carla story, I felt a sense of moral agency as I and others worked with her.

In the school system testing episode, the moral horizons were set by government and school system policies. I did not agree with them and felt no sense of moral agency. I was expected to be a technician, enacting what was predetermined by others above me in the conduit. My knowledge as a well-educated, experienced teacher was not even considered in the situation. Even though I morally could not support the practice, there was no space for me to refute it. I was left with the dilemma of whether to teach my students the testing game. This is a high-stakes dilemma. If I teach my students and they do well, I increase the position of those who have faith in the testing program. On the other hand, if I do not teach my students the game, they lose and I face the wrath of the parents and the school system. There is a serious downside to either way I manage this dilemma. I left the school system testing meeting feeling defeated. And the story and the helpless character I am in it nag me in my daily work with students in my classroom. The testing dilemma remains unresolved.

CONCLUSION

As a teacher, I live in two places on the professional knowledge landscape: my classroom, where I meet students face-to-face, and places outside my classroom, where I meet all those things that are expected of me. In my classroom, I have a measure of moral freedom as I respond to dilemmas that present themselves. I am a moral agent who can have a shaping effect on situations. I am in charge of my own responses and can influence others' responses to particular situations. But outside my classroom my experience may be quite different. Often things like the testing mandate are delivered to me as a "rhetoric of conclusions" (Schwab, 1962) and I have no access to the inquiry that produced them. Frequently these "rhetorics" conflict with previous rhetorics that have come down the tubes. Yet I am expected to embrace mandates, even conflicting ones, and enact them as if they did not conflict, and as if they were my own. But they are not my own; I have experienced no agency in their production. Rather, I have been an instrument being used to do someone else's bidding.

Many tough situations present themselves within the context of my classroom, situations that tire me. They are not, however, the situations which morally wear me down. The situations that tear at the heart of my practice are the ones in which I am stripped of voice and agency. They are the situations in which someone else's knowledge is delivered to me through the conduit in one place in my professional knowledge landscape and I am expected to enact it as if it were my own in my classroom, another place on my landscape. Living in these two places creates the ongoing, uneasy tensions I have difficulty naming in my practice. It creates the dilemmas that gnaw at my soul.

CHAPTER 3

Personal and Professional Knowledge Landscapes: A Matrix of Relations

F. Michael Connelly and D. Jean Clandinin

The current research interest in teachers' lives represents a dramatic shift in how teaching and its relationship to curriculum and instruction are conceived. Though at first glance the shift may seem to be only one of phenomenon resulting in new knowledge of a new topic, it is much more than that. It is a shift in perspective in which common terms are reshaped. Teaching, for instance, becomes something other than a teacher-student relationship for the transmission of knowledge, and the creation of meaning for students; more than something that can be independently assessed, studied, and improved through skill training. It becomes a component of teachers' professional lives to be understood, as is any aspect of life, in terms of its significance and value in an ongoing narrative of personal and social experience.

Furthermore, while the shift is clearly an epistemological one representing a redefinition of a worthwhile problem of educational knowledge, it is also a moral one representing a shift in the moral landscape of inquiry. It takes only a few hours of reading the literature to see how intimately connected are moral and epistemological matters. People speak passionately for and against certain problems of knowledge, engage in a politics of inquiry (Eisner, 1988), and thereby interweave knowledge and value. The arguments over the appropriateness of studying teachers' lives are as laced with moral admonition as they are constructed of value-independent reason. It cannot be otherwise, though there is a popular fiction that problems of inquiry are strictly problems of knowledge and method.

These observations, of course, apply to the lives of researchers concerned about the shift in inquiry to teachers' lives. The reason we stress the point is that it is, perhaps, easier for us researchers to see the link between knowledge and value in our own lives than it is to see this relationship for teachers' lives, and it is teachers' lives we wish to discuss. We want to make the case that the study of teachers' lives is concerned with knowledge, for teachers individually and collectively. For this work teachers' personal practical knowledge names the former and teachers' professional knowledge landscape names the latter.

These teams make evident the shift in perspective referred to above. The words *teacher, knowledge,* and *profession* remain but shift in meaning. Teachers become active agents, pulling themselves into the future with their own inevitable social agendas, rather than passive agents merely pushed into the future by others' social agendas; they become knowing persons with their own epistemological relations to their milieu and to their students, rather than persons merely responsible for transmitting socially valued knowledge; and knowledge becomes the embodied forms (e.g., images, metaphors, personal philosophy, rhythms, rules, and principles) by which teachers interact with the world, rather than the knowledge of things (e.g., of subject matter, children, and instructional method) that teachers need to know to fulfill their social function. Knowledge becomes, as well, teachers' epistemological relationship to the professional landscape in which they live, rather than the professional markers used by agencies for teacher certification purposes and by teacher professional organizations to win professional status for teacher members.

The unenlightened eye might overlook the significance of the shift in perspective because the terms remain the same while the language and arguments appear as dialects. But underneath, differences are significant, if not profound, and the basic map of relationships between the key terms and people is shifted. Elsewhere, we likened the shift we are discussing to the shift that occurs from thinking in Plato's terms and then in Dewey's inverted Platonism, where the base of Plato's reality pyramid is at the top (Clandinin & Connelly, 1992).

The preamble given in the preceding paragraphs is important because we wish to discuss communal aspects of teachers' knowledge and doing so positions us in a literature of professional knowledge. But our approach to teachers' communal knowledge reflects our focus on teachers' lives. We are not, therefore, directly concerned with many of the matters currently found in the burgeoning literature of teacher professionalism.

Our interest is to explore the knowledge context in which teachers' personal practical knowledge of school and classroom life exists. Chapter 1 developed the idea of in- and out-of-classroom places on the professional knowledge landscape. We focused on the ongoing relationship teachers have with knowledge funneled into the school system for the purpose of altering teachers' classroom lives. We argued that teachers' interaction with this knowledge led to a theory-practice dilemma in teachers' professional lives in which sacred social stories of school change are in conflict with the secret stories of classroom life. We made the case that these epistemological dilemmas were also moral dilemmas. Teachers' knowledge, whether in or out of the classroom, is morally oriented. Dilemmas of knowledge are also moral dilemmas. We wish to pick up this theme in this chapter.

We intend, as well, to broaden our range of consideration of the professional knowledge landscape. We will sketch out the importance of everyday life, personal history, social history, and the moral role of other teachers in the determination of teachers' professional knowledge landscapes.

This multiplicity of moral sources can lead to fragmentation, both in our account of it and in the lives of teachers undergoing the experience. We shall try to hold on to the idea of the narrative construction of a life to retain a semblance of unity in our own account; and we shall argue that teachers' professional knowledge landscapes are morally fragmented and that it is the sense of a professional life with a personal and social narrative history and imagined future that creates whatever order and unity teachers are able to muster. Some, of course, are overwhelmed by the fragmentation and dilemmas, lose their sense of professional identity, and resign their teaching positions. Others maintain a sense of professional identity and work on. Part of our purpose is to better understand the conditions that encourage the necessary sense of professional identity.

We believe that teachers' professional lives take shape in and on a landscape of morally oriented professional knowledge. We also believe that this professional knowledge landscape is in intimate interaction with what one might call landscapes of the personal, outside the professional setting. These settings, each understood in terms of personal and social narratives of experience, weave a matrix of storied influence over one another. Teachers' lives take certain shapes because of their professional knowledge landscape. They draw on their individual biographies, on the particular histories of the professional landscape in which they find themselves, on how they are positioned on the landscape, and on the form of everyday school life that the professional landscape allows. Furthermore, the everyday personal life of the teacher off the professional landscape influences the life on the landscape. Conversely, teachers' professional life on the landscape influences their personal life off the landscape. For example, in our earlier work we showed how the everyday-life rhythms of one teacher, Stephanie, took on a certain shape in her professional knowledge landscape. Stephanie was a primary-division teacher in an inner-city Toronto school, Bay Street School. In a detailed case study, Clandinin (1986) showed how Stephanie's classroom practices were an expression of her image of classroom as home. We also showed how her Jewish life rhythms were expressed in classroom celebrations of all children's special cultural and religious holidays. Likewise, the professional knowledge landscape of Bay Street School, with its particular cycles and rhythms, influenced Stephanie's everyday life as she took her own religious holidays at times that conflicted with specific cycles in the school year (Clandinin & Connelly, 1986). She encouraged gardening units at school and used plants for home and yard decoration. Often her school curriculum was a place to inquire into things of personal interest to her, and vice versa.

To properly understand the professional knowledge landscape, it is necessary to understand it narratively as a changing landscape with a history of its own. Dewey (1938), recent narrativists such as Carr (1986), and we in our work on personal practical knowledge (Connelly & Clandinin, 1988) have shown how communities have a kind of organic integrity. This makes it possible, even necessary, to understand communities as entities with a life history. Most schools, for example, have formal historical records. Stories circulate about the changing nature of the school as it responds to changes in the local community and to society at large and as teachers and administrators come, leave, and are replaced by others. Much of what the school stands for at any one point in time is understandable only in terms of this changing professional landscape. Indeed, the landscape is a kind of archaeological site for epistemological and moral reconstructions. Thus, it is not only that teachers have a professional life on the professional knowledge landscape. The landscape has a life as well. Teachers who live their lives on the professional knowledge landscape shape the landscape over time and the landscape shapes them.

A brief sketch of a partial account of one school's landscape may give a sense of what we mean. Over our past 10 or more years of involvement with one school, we have seen a shift in the school's professional knowledge landscape. We note the shift by searching back through the principals' and teachers' stories of their experiences on the landscape. When we first came to know the school, the principal lived and told a story of the school as a "demonstration" school. The principal had a view of the landscape as a place in which teachers had expert practices that could be demonstrated to other teachers and to preservice teachers. Usually these practices were the ones prescribed as innovative by various researchers and theoreticians. For example, when writing researchers began to describe new ways to understand the writing process, innovation and change experts began to prescribe certain practices as exemplary ones.

These were the practices in teaching writing that were demonstrated for others. A particular professional knowledge landscape was established.

Later, a new principal came to the school, teachers left, and new teachers joined the staff. A story of the school as a "lighthouse" school began to shape the professional knowledge landscape. The stories of the demonstration of expert practices shifted to stories of inquiry into what might be seen as appropriate practices for the context. Teachers were encouraged to engage in an open kind of teaching-as-inquiry where practice was always undergoing change. The story was no longer one of demonstrating what innovators outside the classroom saw as expert practice but became a story of inquiry into practice. Teachers no longer saw themselves as experts in particular strategies and techniques who could serve as models of excellence and certainty for others. Rather, they now began to story themselves as teacher researchers whose ongoing inquiry was the site of new insights and new understandings of practice. Of course, at any one time, as in any archaeological site, there were teachers who still lived and told stories that had been shaped by a professional knowledge landscape ordered by the demonstration-school story and others who lived and told stories shaped by a professional knowledge ordered by the lighthouse-school story. All practices were going on at all times as the horizons of the professional knowledge landscape gradually shifted as teachers came and left and, in their moves, further shaped the landscape and were shaped by it.

Furthermore, the landscape of nonprofessional everyday life also changes epistemologically and morally over time. It has its own narrative history. The professional knowledge landscape and its moral history, individuals and their moral histories, and the morality of everyday life and its moral history are an interactive matrix out of which a teacher or group of teachers become who they are as professionals.

As we look back on the lives of early teachers in Alberta, we see how different this general matrix of relationships was compared with our understanding of it now. For example, an early Alberta teacher, Michael's mother, Marion Connelly, began teaching in a one-room rural grade 1–9 school in the 1920s. For Marion, there was a close relationship between the everyday living on the personal landscape and the in-classroom and out-of-classroom places on the professional knowledge landscape.

There were, of course, the rudiments of a conduit. Marion's husband was the trustee and represented the school division. There was an inspector and there was a government department of education. However, Marion's place on the out-of-classroom professional knowledge landscape was, for the most part, continuous with her classroom place on the landscape. There was no staff room. When the inspector arrived, he went to the only place possible, the classroom. Both parts of the professional knowledge landscape, the classroom and the out-of-classroom place, were located in the same place.

On many days, the personal landscape and the professional landscape seemed to be the same landscape. For example, school was occasionally held for blocks of time at the house when the weather made it difficult to heat the school or when Marion was hurt and could not walk or ride to school; the inspector responsible for her evaluations picked raspberries on summer weekends with the family on the ranch; and, in years when Marion did not teach, the teacher boarded at her house. In all three examples the boundary lines in the matrix are blurred.

In her own lifetime, the matrix in which her professional knowledge landscape was embedded shifted dramatically. The school was closed and a centralized grade 1–12 school was formed in which she was a teacher. With this move the out-of-classroom professional knowledge landscape became more apparent and intrusive: Marion had a school principal, was subject to school policy, had divided responsibilities for sports and other social activities, and events such as school concerts and summer softball that the community had organized were now organized by the principal with help from the teachers. As we read the demographic information we also see how dramatically the boundaries of the in- and out-of-classroom professional knowledge landscape shifted. When Marion Connelly began to teach, there was roughly one person outside of the classroom in supervisory, administrative, and consultative positions for every 31 teachers in classrooms. By the 1980s, there was roughly one person outside of the classroom for each 11 teachers in the classroom (Welker, 1992). Later in this chapter, we illustrate how the out-of-classroom place on the professional knowledge landscape of current Alberta teachers is remarkably different from that experienced by teachers like Marion Connelly.

Because the personal landscape, the out-of-classroom place on the professional knowledge landscape, and the in-class knowledge landscape were so intimately interwoven in the matrix, the moral quality of teachers' everyday life was on professional display. Teachers did not just lead good or bad lives; they lived exemplary lives for their students. In effect, the moral aspect of classroom teaching carried over into teachers' personal lives. Codes of appearance and behavior in everyday life were often specified for teachers in Marion's day. Teachers, therefore, experienced a kind of reverse moral conduit in which moral expectations for the classroom dictated significant aspects of the moral quality of everyday life.

The narrative evolution of a more clearly demarcated landscape of professional knowledge—both in-classroom and out-of-classroom—and personal living diminished the influence of the reverse conduit. Even matrix situations like Marion's consolidated school, small and intimate by comparison with today's comprehensive urban schools, dramatically shifted her experience of the relationship of personal and professional life as she moved into that school from her one-room country school. Not only was the community less involved in the details of her school's extracurricular existence; it was less pedagogically interested in, and in control of, the moral quality of her personal life. Over the years teacher professional organizations have seen this as a positive aspect of increased professionalism. Indeed, for many, professionalism means the separation of personal from professional landscapes of knowledge and morality. Recently, for example, a local teacher has been much in the media because of his support for an Ontario wing of the Ku Klux Klan. Some want him fired. His main defense, not only by the teachers' organization but by school trustees and others as well, is that there is no evidence that he has brought his racist views into the classroom. Conversely, a recent celebrated case in Alberta led to the firing of a teacher who, it was shown, had taught that the Jewish holocaust was a Jewish cover story. The case hinged on his classroom actions and not on his personal views on the matter, which were well known publicly. With Marion's tightly knit matrix of relationships, these cases would have been unthinkable. If the events had occurred in her time and if she had personally supported the Ku Klux Klan or critics of the Holocaust literature, she would very likely have been summarily fired.

But the demarcation of the various parts of teachers' landscapes also carries consequences with which proponents of professionalism have reason for concern. Consider that Marion's early Alberta story also relates to the in-classroom place on the professional knowledge landscape. We earlier described classrooms as a secret place on the professional knowledge landscape: a place where teachers were partially insulated from the conduit (though this secret place is now under constant bombardment). When the professional knowledge landscape and the personal landscape of the teacher came as closely together as they did in Marion's one-room school, the whole community knew what was going on in the classroom. Mostly, the classroom functioned then, as now, as a secret place where teachers and students interacted. But because the community knew what was happening behind that classroom door, Marion's were very public secrets. Parents knew what Marion was doing, but they rarely if ever visited, nor did they interfere. If there was trouble in the classroom the parents, by and large, supported Marion.

Current attempts to open classrooms to their communities are efforts to make public secrets of classroom secrets. There is more in this than mere control and more than nostalgia for a time like Marion's. The strengthened professionalism of teaching (Schön, 1983) has run a narrative course of conflict with the historical sense of relationship between school and community. Now teachers sense that making classroom secrets public and opening the classroom to the community would open it to the multiple interpretations, criticisms, and requirements of the conduit. Though not new, the conduit is now a far more disruptive narrative influence than it was in Marion's day. Teachers sense that if today's classroom secrets became public secrets, the matrix of relationships is such as to pit the community against the teachers. They know this would ensue from the judgments that would inevitably follow as various leaders applied the rhetoric of conclusions flowing from the conduit to an assessment of teachers' classroom lives. The conflict the teachers sense is not so much a we-them but the multiplicity of competing moral positions that reflect the modern complex of forces that influence the professional knowledge landscape.

Teachers who have worked with us note that they have become accustomed to turning their attention upward as they step out of the classroom into the out-of-classroom place on the professional knowledge landscape. They look to see what new prescriptions, new mandates, and new policies are dropping from the conduit to litter the professional knowledge landscape. On the landscape outside the classroom, teachers become attentive to the many moral admonitions raining down from above. However, in some of the schools where we now work, teachers tell us that parents are very much part of what was the secret act of teaching. They now are a part of the professional knowledge landscape in the classroom. Parents sit at the back of classrooms to observe teaching, work with groups of children, and become involved with individual students. Their presence in the classroom raises the possibility of competing moral positions on teaching in the classroom. In one school we know of, parents had been welcome participants in the classroom. Parents came to value and like the strong language arts, fine arts, science, and physical education programs. However, they thought the mathematics program was inadequate and, without consulting the teachers, figured out that outside expert involvement would be useful. A group of parents who had been most involved in the classroom contacted an outside expert from a nearby university who suggested he had ways to improve the classroom. A meeting was called for teachers and parents and the teachers found themselves trying to explain to parents and to the outside expert that changing the classroom curriculum in ways the expert was suggesting would radically alter the entire program. The expert's suggestion was experienced by the teachers as something also filtering down the conduit. But the prescription was introduced into the professional knowledge landscape by parents and was fed directly into the classroom place on the professional knowledge landscape. The parents, who had come to see the curriculum as comprised of a collection of individual subject-matter courses, acted in what they saw as a way to improve the classroom instruction. Asking for expert assistance for the teachers in what the parents saw as a weaker subject-matter area seemed to them a positive move. In the parents' narratives of experience, in the curriculum guidelines, and in the provincial assessment practices, subject matter was treated as discrete units. Parents imagined their participation would be a positive moral force. What the teachers experienced was a new and competing moral force on the in-classroom place on the professional knowledge landscape. The parents' actions opened up a competing moral position that had the potential to radically change the teaching in the classroom. What becomes evident in this story from the professional knowledge landscape of today's teachers is that there are many moral forces in and out of the classroom shaping teachers' lives.

It is not uncommon for certain teachers and communities nowadays to experience a matrix of close relationships. The situations we have in mind look, for all intents and purposes, similar to Marion's, where the boundary lines between school and community are close and blurred. Cheryl Craig's story of Carla in Chapter 2 is illustrative of the interweaving of the professional knowledge landscape of the classroom, the out-of-classroom professional knowledge landscape, and the personal knowledge landscape. As told, Craig's grade-3 classroom teaching comfortably coincides with stories in the out-of-classroom professional knowledge landscape about good teaching. The story begins with a secure sense of teacher identity due to the harmonious relationship between the in-classroom and out-of-classroom professional knowledge landscapes. Subsequently, Craig's story suggests frequent exchanges between her classroom and the community as her new student, Carla, so different from other students in Craig's classroom and from a home with parents transient to the community and in socioeconomic circumstances very different from those of others in the community, is fitted into classroom and school life. Craig's teenage son, for example, came to the school for special sessions with Carla and, later, volunteer parents participated in a similar role. Furthermore, teachers, other parents, and other children worked together in an apparently easy mutuality to brighten Carla's academic and social life. The fact that Craig is confident in her sense that she is doing what is expected according to school stories and that she is able to involve her personal life in the classroom through the efforts of her son and to work with the community and other teachers throughout the school on behalf of Carla is reminiscent of Marion's one-room school setting. In an important sense there are similarities. The matrix of relationships between the in-classroom and the out-of-classroom places on the professional knowledge landscape and the personal landscape is similar for Marion and for Cheryl. In both cases an intimate relationship with blurred boundary lines is evident.

But, we believe, the moral authority for the intimacy of the relationship is dramatically different in the two cases. In Marion's case, moral authority is given by the matrix itself. It is the intimacy of the matrix that creates her identity as a teacher and the confidence that goes with knowing that one is doing what one is expected to do. Following Taylor (1989), knowing where one stands in the matrix of the relationships is what makes for a moral identity and the professional confidence that goes with it. But a careful reading of Craig's story reveals that she stands in a very different relationship to the matrix of relationships than does Marion. Storied clues to her different position in the matrix are scattered throughout the narrative. Craig "recognized a tension between the school story and the life story Carla brought to the school." Craig adapted her teaching to suit Carla's needs and became "strategically lenient" with her. But this classroom adaptation was done at a cost to her sense of identity as a teacher. Carla, Craig notes, was being monitored. Craig's classroom was situated in such a way that it was often on public view and she worried at how her teaching would be perceived given the monitoring and her knowledge that parent groups had "scrutinized particular staff members and students in the past." Indeed, some parents argued that Carla should not be in the school and, as Craig adapted her teaching to Carla, she worried that this possibly would provide evidence for parents who wanted Carla removed.

It is clear from these concerns that Craig's moral authority as a teacher is not given by her place in the matrix, but rather that the relational quality of the matrix and her place in it are the results of something else. Craig works hard, in fact, to adjust the matrix to her purposes and writes that "something happened" when she put parent volunteers in tutorial contact with Carla. But suppose Craig's efforts hadn't "worked"? Carla could have been removed from the school and Craig could have been reprimanded, removed from the school, or even fired, or at least so she thought. What does this signify about the matrix? The actions against Carla and Craig would have been taken by the parents in consultation with those in authority. In effect, action would have been taken via the conduit. From this it is clear that the moral authority for Craig's sense of identity and for the intimacy of the matrix of relationships is given by the conduit. In one of the most sacred of sacred stories, it is often said that "the Lord giveth and the Lord taketh away." In the sacred story of theory-practice relationships the quality of the relationships among the in-classroom place on the professional knowledge landscape, the out-of-classroom place on the professional knowledge landscape, and the personal knowledge landscape is given by the conduit. It may be given in one form, taken away, and formed anew. We believe that, for the most part, present day teachers who work in apparently intimate matrix relationships such as Craig's understand that at some important level it is not the same as it once was in situations such as Marion's. Their landscapes of professional knowledge are radically different and their sense of identity, confidence, and self-worth as teachers is given in a very different way. They stand in a fundamentally different relationship to the matrix of relationships that bear on teachers' epistemological and moral landscapes.

PART II

PROFESSIONAL KNOWLEDGE LANDSCAPES OF TEACHER EDUCATION

CHAPTER 4

Shifting Moral Landscapes: A Story of Sonia's Teacher Education

D. Jean Clandinin and Pat Hogan

We first met Sonia at Jude McCullough's school when we were planning an alternative program in teacher education (Clandinin, Davies, Hogan, & Kennard, 1993). Sonia was a second-year education student and a good friend of Jude's. When we first talked with her, she often storied herself as a parent and as a parent volunteer. Sonia and Jude, a primary-division teacher, had begun their friendship when Jude taught Sonia's children several years earlier. Sonia's stories often revolved around themes of being a dutiful daughter, a good mother, a hard worker, a concerned parent. She was heavily involved as a parent volunteer in Jude's classroom and became the volunteer coordinator in the school. One account Sonia gave of herself was when she described an upcoming interview for a teacher-aide position with the same principal who had worked with her when she was a parent volunteer and when she worked as a student teacher with Jude.

> The principal has seen me excel in a lot of things with the parent groups and with key communicators [parent contacts] and she's the one that nominated me for that Lamp of Learning award. You know she's seen me excel in a lot of things and I wasn't confident in my role as a teacher because it's a new thing and I want to be so good at it but it's just like life and death or something that maybe I wouldn't be as good as a teacher as I was at my other roles. You know, she probably thought I was a very good parent. She probably thought I was very good in those other roles. (Conversation, August 18, 1992)

Even after she has been recognized as very capable in these other roles, she still doubts her teaching ability. During Sonia's work as a parent volunteer with Jude, Jude noticed how Sonia worked with children and with parents. She began to encourage Sonia to become a teacher. Initially Sonia resisted, claiming she was not smart enough to be a teacher. Sonia had difficulty believing she was smart enough to be a teacher even though she had taught at an after-school language program. She described her work as a Ukrainian teacher in the following way.

> Some letters from the parents of the kids that I teach at Ukrainian school blew me away with how they talk. I keep thinking why? I'm not doing anything special or different and they're saying "Do you think you'll teach again next year even if you get a teaching job?" or "Can you please teach?" or "She didn't want to come to Ukrainian school and now she wants to and I don't want her to think that you're not going to be here next year." And just that their kids are really happy and I know that they're happy in their learning but the biggest thing is that they want to come to Ukrainian school and to go to Ukrainian school on a Wednesday night. I think, if I can make kids want to do that, then I'm okay, you know? (Conversation, August 18, 1992)

When we asked Sonia how she first became involved in teaching Ukrainian school once a week, she described herself as not really able to teach.

> I felt really uncomfortable doing it because I don't speak Ukrainian that well, not like a teacher should speak Ukrainian but I felt comfortable because she [the person who hired her] said "The children you'll be teaching are children that don't speak Ukrainian at home." So I thought I could relate to them there because my kids don't speak Ukrainian at home. I don't speak Ukrainian at home. I've been through Ukrainian school for years and years as a student so I know what it's like when they expect the same thing from everybody even though all your home lives are so different. So I felt like I could relate to these kids and make it fun for them. I really felt that it was important that they could feel Ukrainian without having to necessarily speak it perfectly. . . . I guess she was really happy from how the parents were talking about their kids enjoying Ukrainian school and wanting to come to Ukrainian school and that kind of made me come back again even though I really didn't feel like I belonged because a lot of these people that were teaching had teaching degrees and were teaching Ukrainian school on the side. (Conversation, August 18, 1992)

Even with feedback from parents, Sonia found it difficult to tell a story of herself as a good teacher. She still storied herself as less competent in her subject-matter knowledge of the language and as not having the recognition of her ability through having a teaching degree.

Eventually, through her connection with Jude, Sonia felt confident enough to enroll at the university in a Bachelor of Education program. She was in her second year of the program when a group of schoolteachers and university teachers began to plan a collaborative alternative program for the third-year Bachelor of Education program. Jude was heavily involved in the planning process as a member of the steering committee. The alternative program was planned to allow teachers, student teachers, and university teachers to work closely together. One reason for Jude's excitement about the proposed program was that she saw the possibility for Sonia to complete her third year of the program and her practicum in the context of continuing their relationship with each other.

Sonia's experience of the alternative program came as a surprise to her. She was surprised to find that her university teachers were interested in what she had to say. She began to feel comfortable with and to accept the possibility that she might have knowledge.

> I think when we were in our practicum I found it a shock sometimes that the teachers... would listen and be interested in what I was saying or saying "Wow" or this or that and it took a long time to kind of feel comfortable, thinking that maybe what I was saying was good .... (Conversation, July 26, 1991)

In the above quotation Sonia gave the sense that she was awakening (Connelly & Clandinin, 1994) to a sense of herself as a knowing person. She began to tell a tentative story of herself as one who knows. What we saw ourselves doing in the alternative program was moving outside the traditional hierarchial story of knowledge as generated in the university and delivered to teachers and student teachers *to* a more collaborative program in which all voices were valued. It was, in some ways, an attempt to create a different moral landscape for teacher education.

At the completion of the alternative program, Sonia seemed to anticipate that she would continue to be able to live and tell a story of herself as a knowing person in her final year of the Bachelor of Education program. She heard the same constructivist language that she had heard in the alternative program at the beginning of her fourth year of university studies. As the following quotation illustrates, Sonia's sense of a continuation of a story within the reset moral horizons of another story was short-lived.

> But when we first started we tried to get into his class [one of the fourth-year university teachers] he sounded really positive, that his class is really different. "Well that's good, I think you'll fit in being from the alternative program" and when he started he'd say "I'm not going to be feeding you information, I want you to internalize and it's going to be you will kind of write about what you want to write." It kind of gives a feeling that it might be a little bit of what we were doing last year. It started out feeling that way but as the course went, you got the feeling that there was a certain way to do things even though he kept saying "No, that's why I'm being so vague because I want you to figure it out the way you want to do it or write the way you want." But then he'd come back and say "I didn't know how to feel because some of you did it this way and some of you did it this way and I must have been too vague and I feel like I've failed" and it went back to "Yeah there must be a certain way to do this." (Conversation, July 26, 1991)

Sonia, in the fourth year of her teacher education program, found herself back within the sacred theory-practice story but now she experienced the horizons of the sacred story as a loss. She had started to live and tell a new story of herself as a knowing person and when this was no longer valued by her university teachers she felt helpless. She described her sense of this in the following transcript.

> It kind of creates that helpless feeling again. You don't feel like you can think for yourself. It's almost like they're going to be giving you everything you need to know and you do kind of get, not get lazy but just you get that "you're not the one that knows anymore." They know and you have to find out everything they know or you'll never get it. (Conversation, July 26, 1991)

It was not that Sonia was not making connections with what she heard from her fourth-year university teachers. For example, in the following quotation she described a feeling of connection. She was still able to make sense of the concepts and strategies that were being explained to her.

> I feel like I can see myself in those words or see my actions in those words. And it's not just, well okay I'm writing a paper and this is what a teacher does and this is what should happen in the classroom. I'm not just saying them. I believe in those things. I've done those things. You know, like that right brain thing that I wrote

> about. She [a university teacher] was going through that list and I was thinking that I've always wanted to do music in the classroom . . . and she said "and Baroque music is really good because of the heart beat" and all that stuff and I'm going that's the kind of music I like, that's the kind of music that I play. I just have a sense of having it in my classroom, I don't know how, but that's going to be my classroom. And here they're saying that's a wonderful thing. That it stimulates all those neurons or whatever, and touching the child on the head. I always do that. I always touch on the head and I've noticed it a lot with Josh [a child with whom she has been working as she attends class]. I'd touch him on the head. I'd stroke his back. Just that kind of touch and it would also be so calming . . . I do that. Smiles. I do that. Humor, I do that. All these things she was saying. But all of a sudden hearing this big shot guy who is like really, really, really, smart saying okay, these are the things you can do. I've proven it with all my research and everything. I'm just always really scared of these people, they are so smart and they are able to articulate and they are able to . . . Like I really feel like they know and I don't feel like that at all. (Conversation, March 28, 1991)

In the opening line there was a sense of Sonia's recognition of a connection between her lived story and what she was hearing in her university classes: "I feel like I can see myself in those words or see my actions in those words." Her words, however, conveyed a sense of the unexpected, for she had come to know that the professional knowledge landscape of the university created by the sacred theory-practice story was usually one in which she silenced her own stories as she wrote papers or talked about "what should happen." She knew that the landscape of the university was one that prescribed the story a teacher was supposed to tell. There was a sense that she understood that the prescribed story was a moral one as she said, "This is what should happen in the classroom." She became aware of the moral horizons of the landscape within which she was situated when she listened to one of her teacher education instructors tell her what was appropriate. She took the instructor's words and used them to project herself into the future ("but that's just going to be my classroom") at the same time that she thought about her current work as a classroom aide with a grade-1 child, Josh.

Connecting to the words of the university instructor in this way surprised her, for she had seen theorists as "really scary" and as "knowing." She had now begun to see herself somewhat differently in relation to theory, a tenuous view as she described herself seeing university teachers as knowing and herself as not feeling "like that at all." Reflecting on her experience of the alternative program and her fourth-year experience, she began to question her story of herself as a teacher:

> So this year has kind of made me just realize that maybe I do know a few things. And maybe I do know a few things that I need to become a teacher. Maybe they are not the kind of things that will get me good marks but I think everyone keeps telling me these things or trying to point out these things in me and maybe I'm just trying to see some of them. That they are there. . . . I think that I've got what it takes to be a teacher but I can still be kind of swept away with the feelings I get at university. Like I don't know or that I'm not smart enough to be a teacher. You know. (Conversation, March 28, 1991)

As she questioned herself, she began to awaken to a new story of herself. This was not the story valued on the university professional knowledge landscape, where university teachers valued something else for "good marks." Coming to tell a story of herself as someone who had "what it takes to be a good teacher" was difficult, situated as she was within a landscape that could "sweep her away" with a sense that she did not know or was not smart enough to be a teacher. In the following quotation, she looked back to try to tell her story of teacher education.

> Because that is what I went in with when I first started. I was going to be taught how to be a teacher. I was going to go and after I left I would know everything I needed to know as a teacher. But even then, like Jude would even say "You know you have got what it takes to be a teacher. You're going to go, they'll give you the tools that you need or whatever." I don't know how she explained it but she said "But right now you have what it takes." But I still went into it thinking, okay, they'll teach me. I'll become really smart and then I'll be a teacher. . . . And sometimes I still think like, I've only got two months left, I don't know everything yet. And that's why I picked up that math course, I thought this is my last chance. I still don't feel like I am ready for this. . . . So since it's my last three months here, I'll pick up this math course. (Conversation, March 28, 1991)

When she started she was deeply rooted in the sacred story, that is, that she would be given knowledge from the university teachers about how to teach. Even comments such as those of her friend/teacher Jude were not enough to allow her to begin to tell a new story. Even at the end of her degree program, she lived the character of teacher in the sacred story as she signed on for one more course. There was a sense that living the sacred story would fill her with the knowledge she "needs to become a teacher."

As she underwent her experiences in teacher education, she tried to believe the story told to her by Jude and her teachers in the alternative program that she had "what it takes to be a teacher." Her fourth-year university experiences only served to convince her that she didn't "know enough" or she wasn't "smart enough" to be a teacher. In many ways, her fourth-year university experience, situated within the sacred theory-practice story, had left her feeling that she could never know everything. She felt there was much to be learned from the experts. She sought out another math course as a "last chance."

Sonia struggled with wanting to name the sacred theory-practice story and was troubled and uncertain.

> Like I think I realized that deep down that they're not going to teach me everything I need to learn about being a teacher and I'm not going to learn everything this year and be all set to go next year but I guess when I compare myself to what I see around me and the products, then I get a sense that maybe that shows something in this whole scheme of things and it's very hard for me to do that kind of stuff and to get through it. I'm doing good in my marks and I'm doing really well in my math course and that's the same kind of course as, like I say, with the journal writing and everything, so I'm not having any problems but there's one course that's really making me doubt myself . . . Language Arts and not being able to write pages and pages. Like write an observation on one page, write a reflection two pages long. My reflection sometimes is like three sentences. Not three sentences but it's like maybe just a page, right. But that's all I see in it. It's a really important reflection to me but all I can see is a bloody page worth. But I'm sure there is more in there that I could talk some more about or if someone looked at it, they'd be able to see something else. I feel that I don't measure up because of the amount written or whether I can say it in the right ways or quote the right theories or whatever, like I feel that part is missing. I don't know how important that part is from the whole thing. (Conversation, March 28, 1991)

In this quotation, Sonia struggled with "the right ways" or quoting "the right theories," things that would acknowledge that she was a good teacher as evidenced by her knowledge landscape. She struggled, caught between trusting her own storied knowledge and living out the expected story. We saw Sonia standing within the moral horizon established by the sacred theory-practice story of teacher education but sensing that this was not an authentic horizon that fit with her life. What started to become apparent here was that Sonia had a sense that the sacred theory-practice story was not a story to live by. She understood that the story of knowledge as hierarchical was not the story that she must live in teaching. But in recognizing this, she acknowledged the tension. As she tried to name the inauthenticity of the moral horizons established by the sacred theory-practice story, she began to doubt where she stood and what she knew.

> Maybe now it's the position I'm in where it's marks and marks, exams and marks, papers . . . sometimes I think I'd love to sit back in his class and not write down every word he says. But to me I figure that's the only way I'm going to get everything down that I'll need to know to write a paper or I need for an exam because I don't like listening or learning that way. And I felt wouldn't it be nice just to sit back and take in all this stuff and really enjoy what he has to say because he knows an awful lot of stuff. And he brings a lot of stuff for us to read and to think about but I can't do it in that kind of way. Not relax and listen. (Conversation, March 28, 1991)

Her experience in the university situated in a professional knowledge landscape bounded by the sacred theory-practice story made her feel uncomfortable, filled with tension. She wanted to sit back and think about different possibilities in what she was learning but the horizons of the story were set out by the evaluation system. These horizons kept her focused on "writing down every word he says."

Sonia recalled her experience in the alternative program in teacher education where we sought to make visible the sacred theory-practice story through questioning the hierarchical nature of knowledge and relationships as we sought to establish more collaborative relationships between and among university teachers, cooperating teachers, and student teachers. Sonia had begun to tell a story of herself as having personal practical knowledge, constructed and reconstructed as she lived and told her stories and relived and retold them in conversations with others and with theory. She had begun to recognize herself within a particular moral landscape. Now back within a moral landscape established by the sacred story, she found herself facing questions.

> The instructor said that the program that I was in was great. That it gave me a voice but a drawback is that it has got me writing in

> such a way that it's hard for me now to include theory in it . . . . And the instructor said, "obviously you've been able to find your voice and it's great but unfortunately it's not working in that you'll find it difficult now to talk with the theory and the theory is important. You need that theory." (Conversation, March 28, 1991)

Sonia was confused by the shifting moral landscape and found it very difficult to respond to a university teacher who lived within the horizons established by the sacred theory-practice story.

Part of the confusion for Sonia was her recognition that, in some ways, she and fellow students from the alternative program threatened the fourth-year university teachers. As a student and as a mother/volunteer, she was accustomed to feeling threatened by experts, whether university teachers, teachers, or principals. To understand herself as posing a threat to someone she storied above her in the hierarchy was new for her. One instance in which she saw herself posing a threat was when students from the alternative program wanted to work together.

> I felt that he hated us sitting together. That was a weird thing with him and one time when Jeannie [another student from the alternative program] came and wasn't put in a group [because she missed a class] he said "As long as you don't go with Sonia." (Conversation, July 26, 1991)

Another recognition that somehow they posed a threat was when she and her classmates wanted to listen to experienced school teachers' stories within the class. It seemed threatening to their university teacher that they could learn from each other, and particularly that they could learn from the stories of teachers.

> People like Fran [an experienced school teacher studying with Sonia's preservice class] who were really good with what they were doing, sometimes when she'd talk or sometimes when she'd read a piece of hers, I think I could learn so much from her and it was almost as if it was threatening in a way to the university teacher and it's too bad that we couldn't maybe learn more from those teachers who had a lot to offer. Fran was really outspoken so she'd sit there and talk and she was an incredible teacher. I think if she would have been up there a few times we could have learned a lot with her approach with kids and different problems and just, she was so sincere and caring for kids. (Conversation, July 26, 1991)

In the next quotation Sonia provided insight into how she was making sense of the shifting horizons.

> I think I have theory but I guess if I don't sit there and quote and spout off about it every paragraph, then I guess I don't have theory. If I don't start by going quotation marks with the dots and everything, then I guess I don't have theory . . . . I guess the university teacher thinks it's really important to be able to talk about the theory. I know at one point the teacher said it's good if you have the names and everything. If you go and talk to a principal or whatever, half the time they won't even know these guys but at least you'll be accountable and they know you know your stuff because you've got . . . so I found it really hard and I agreed with the university teacher. I found it hard to pull it in maybe because I couldn't talk about those theorists in the way that I talk in my paper yet and by just sticking them in, it didn't feel like my paper. It took away from being an observation and a reflection. It went more to a normal kind of paper. And so maybe that is a problem with me but I don't think so. (Conversation, May 2, 1991)

Sonia understood the conflicting stories of theory-practice for she saw theory as part of what she knew—not as separate from her knowing but as informing her knowing. The reason she was given for knowing theory as part of the sacred theory-practice story was to make her "accountable." Even as she recognized that her lived story belied this, she agreed with the teacher. Perhaps the university teacher was right even though Sonia again recognized that her work would not "feel like my paper" and that it would be "more to a normal kind of paper."

> I guess he's given us so much and so he's just given us sprinklings of all of these things. I don't feel confident spouting off about a lot of this stuff. I get the gist of what he's talking about and the more I read and the more I research for my papers then I get a better understanding of it but I told him maybe I don't feel confident yet to sit there and to spout it back to you. (Conversation, May 2, 1991)

Sonia, overwhelmed by the changing stories of how she should relate to theory, began to lose a sense of herself and felt silenced, blaming herself for not feeling "confident yet." She returned to reflecting on how she had written her papers the year before in the alternative program, in ways that had authorized her own knowing:

> Well I took a chance to do it like our papers last year because it was observing someone using language or learning language or learning through language or whatever and then writing what we learned from it. The reflection. . . . like this thing was 45 pages. There is a lot of work, a lot of reflection, a lot of talking about it . . . . I had to do the research about all the theorists that he gave us just to see what he might be looking for or whatever. And then just the time it took to try and find observations, you learn from every observation but you're trying to pick something that's going to appeal to him or that might fit into some classification of observations. I don't know. So it was just really a lot of time and effort put into it. (Conversation, May 2, 1991)

After participating in a program that tried to interrupt and question the sacred theory-practice story, Sonia struggled with trying to make sense of what she knew. She ended up saying "I don't know." What she found herself doing made no sense at all to her. She no longer had a sense of who she was in her university courses and little sense of where she stood in relation to the sacred story. She ended by saying, "So it was just really a lot of time and effort put into it."

> The whole feeling I got from not knowing the theoretical language that will give me the language that is shared among professionals and colleagues and that will allow me to talk to them . . . to more or less feel as if I won't be able to talk to them. You know, once I finish these four years I assume that I am now going to be a teacher or whatever, so I feel like I should be able to talk to somebody about it but that's how I felt. (Conversation, June 20, 1991)

As she reflected on her student experience, Sonia again felt inadequate. She was concerned that she did not know "the theoretical language that will give me that language that is shared among professionals and colleagues and that will allow me to talk to them." She now began to believe that the language of theory was what she must learn to speak in order to be a teacher. If she could not speak from within the horizons established by the sacred theory-practice story, perhaps she would not be heard. There was a deep sense that Sonia knew that her stories of practice had no place in the discourse of the sacred story. While she felt she "should be able to talk to somebody about it," she was beginning to sense that this telling was impossible.

Part of Sonia's continuing questioning of the moral horizons created by the sacred theory-practice story arose as she participated in the third-year alternative teacher education program and worked with university teachers and cooperating teachers who were trying to live a restoried version of teacher education. But in her final year of teacher education, which was again within the professional knowledge landscape of the university, Sonia also worked as an aide with a special-needs child, Josh. As Sonia worked with Josh in the school, she existed within, but somewhat apart from, the professional knowledge landscape of the school. She also was living within, but somewhat apart from, the professional knowledge landscape of the university. Sonia came to see that much of what she was asked to do within the school professional knowledge landscape and within the university professional knowledge landscape did not fit with the story she and Josh were living together. Sonia talked about how she and Josh came to work together. In the following transcript she describes the story that was told to her prior to beginning her work with him.

> The feeling I got was that they basically needed a bodyguard for the teacher because there was this little boy in the classroom that was scheduled to go into a behavior program in April. But they had to keep him in the school for the month of March but they didn't have the resources like the extra teachers in the school for someone to be with him all the time and he was creating problems in the classroom, for the teacher, for the kids. The vice-principal would be spending half his time running after him, trying to catch him. They said he would run into bathrooms, lock the door. They'd have to get the janitors to unlock it because if they tried going under, he'd kick and throw fits. So when I came that first day I met the resource teacher and the principal and they gave me the background again saying "You have to be very firm." So they painted this picture of this child that was going to bite and kick and run away from me and throw tantrums and told me just take him somewhere, into another room and sit him down and wait until he calms down. Basically do whatever you have to, to keep it at an even keel for the teacher and the other kids. So I was really scared. I'm walking in and I'm thinking, "Oh my God, I won't be able to be the way they want me to be." . . . Because I don't see myself introducing myself or meeting someone under those kinds of circumstances. It didn't sound like me and I just thought I'm going to be in a lot of trouble. First of all I thought this would look good for me [on a resume] and then I thought it probably won't look good for me because this child is going to be all over me and it will prove once and for all to the principal and to everybody else that I'm just too kind and I don't have any discipline and don't have any

> control. I thought all these weaknesses were going to be brought out in vivid color for everyone to see so I thought, I'm in trouble. I really thought I was in trouble. I thought this was stupid, I shouldn't have done this and I was scared. I was in the room, waiting for these kids to come in and every time a little boy came in I was totally petrified that it was this child and then all of a sudden he walked in with the principal and she took him aside and introduced me to him and it was the feeling "Well, this is your boss, you listen to her. She's here so that you don't disrupt this class anymore so you don't . . ." And so I just felt like this wicked witch of the north that's been put there to sit on him so he didn't do anything bad. So we sat down together and I thought I was going to be running after him in about two minutes and he just kept looking at me and every time he looked at me I'd look at him and he'd look away. Then when he wasn't looking at me and I'd be looking at him trying to think "Oh God, what's going on in this kid's mind, what is he really like?" And really, I was so scared of him that first day, I was just petrified. And I just talked to him, we talked about a lot of things almost like things that you would think about in your mind, I would have to think about them out loud so that he knew why we were doing something or why I was asking him to do this or like really spelling things out for him. It seemed he had a lot of the social skills but somehow didn't apply in there. It was like I had to keep reminding him OK don't run up to somebody and barge up at them, things like that. He just needed reminding or something, on how to act around people because I think people were very scared of him or something. (Conversation, March 28, 1991)

Sonia, still doubting whether she has what is necessary to be a teacher, worried about how her work with this child would be storied. However, as she sat with him that first day, she began to understand that his lived story, yet untold, was different from the one constructed for him. Sonia, sensing the possibility of interrupting the school's story of him, began to work with him to help him live a new one.

> It was like his behavior was . . . he wouldn't say hi, he'd kind of meet you with a charge. He'd just pounce at you and that was the whole picture of him. Today the teacher said I can't believe that that is the same kid sitting there. He's so calm. He's taking part in the class. . . . I don't know everything that's in his file but because I've been with him for almost a month, I feel like I know a lot of things about him and know what bothers him and what he can deal with

> and what he can't deal with. I really think that given a little bit more time he could fit in somehow. I don't know what happens in these behavior classes but maybe they'll just kind of give him those skills to be able to come back and be part of the group or be more independent, or whatever, I don't know what they'll do there. But the last week I barely had any time with him. He wouldn't need to talk to me any more, he'd just run and get a game at the math games or go do something with another kid. It was almost as if he could go play with his friends . . . almost like a mother thing. . . . I know you're going to stay there so now I can go have fun. He'd take a lot of initiative on his own. I'd just be surprised or shocked sometimes because a lot of times I'd have to say well why don't you go do this or why don't you go see if there is a book or whatever, but all of a sudden he'd finish his work and it was almost as if he didn't need me as much and he was starting to relate more to the kids around him and do stuff more with them. (Conversation, March 28, 1991)

As Sonia and Josh worked together, Josh began to live a changed story of being part of the class, of being a child who completed his work, of being a friend to other children. But even with this changed story Josh was living, the plans for the institutional story of segregated special education were unfolding. Sonia found herself living out a story with Josh in which their moral horizons were set by others. It no longer mattered what story Sonia and Josh were authoring. Their stories were unheard as he was moved to live his story in the special education class.

The principal and the teacher, despite Sonia's awareness that Josh was increasingly able to live a story within the horizons of acceptability in the school, had already decided to transfer him to a special, segregated setting. Sonia held a strong opinion in a conversation with Pat Hogan that this move was not morally right for Josh.

> He's there Wednesday April 10 and they want me to go with him. And it's really funny. They didn't want to tell him. I asked them Friday when they were going to tell him that I wasn't going to be there because in music we had been singing and I couldn't remember the words and I said to him when we were going to the water fountain, it takes me so long to remember words of songs. Like I have to keep going over and over and over it again. And he said "Don't worry, we've got until the end of grade 1." And I thought "Oh God." I didn't even know what to say because I didn't know what they had said to him and when I talked to them, they had the psy-

> chologist there and everything. They said "Well maybe it's better if we don't say anything to him." You know, like let's wait until the end. Because things are going so well and I guess they just didn't want any flare-up. But when he came to school on Monday his mom brought him and I met her for the first time. And she said to me, "Oh, he really talks about you a lot and he really has become close to you and he says you are his best friend." You know she was really happy and stuff like that. And that morning he told me in our conversation as we were talking, it came out that he found out that I wasn't going to be there any more after Easter. So he was able to handle that. Everybody didn't think he would be able to handle that. But he handled it and he would say a couple of times how he was going to miss me and I said, "Well, we can write letters or I'll give you my phone number and you can phone and tell me what you are doing and how things are going." And so that was okay with him. . . So I'm walking into class and he comes up to me and hands me this yellow sticky with his name and his phone number. Like he really remembers things and everything you tell him is very important to him. That was on his mind and he knew it was the last day and he brought it. (Conversation, March 28, 1991)

As Sonia reflected on her experience with Josh, she was concerned about the part she played in his story. She wondered, in the following transcript, if she needed to voice more forcefully her own sense of what was "right" for Josh.

> It kind of bugs me that maybe I wouldn't have said anything more, if I had been a mouthy person and said, "Look it, I don't think this is right." But maybe I'm thinking two things at once. I wanted to say maybe when I feel more confident when I'm teaching and that's my responsibility and these kids are my responsibility and I feel like that is my responsibility to stand up and be mouthy right, if I see something. And it bugs me when I just said that because one little kid got screwed around because I'm waiting to get this confidence up . . . when I wrote about it in my journal, I kind of had to reflect right, so then I could say that I went with what I felt was better for me but when I did it, like right then, it was just because that's what came out. So maybe because I knew she expected a certain behavior from me, that because I wasn't doing that behavior I felt even more that I wasn't meeting her [the principal's] expectations because I think to me she would feel that then I became a

> teacher. She always said, "I really think she is a good teacher but, you know, she has to be more firm." (Conversation, June 20, 1991)

Lacking the confidence to name herself a good teacher as she finished her teacher education program within the horizons of the sacred theory-practice story, Sonia stated, "I'm waiting to get this confidence up." Within the professional knowledge landscape of the school, she felt she had abandoned her responsibility to Josh because, at the final meeting, she did not tell stories of their work together and instead tried to live up to the expectations set within the principal's story.

This telling of Sonia's story of teacher education helped us to name the power of the sacred theory-practice story and to see the ways in which it established the moral horizons for her lived story. Her work with Jude and others in the alternative program and her work with Josh were experienced as interruptions to the sacred story as Sonia glimpsed possibilities for living and telling her story of learning to teach in new ways.

CHAPTER 5

Learning to Live a Competing Story of Teacher Education

Annie Davies

"I'd like you to be part of a new study into the knowledge contexts in which you work. What do you think?"
"I wouldn't pass up the opportunity for anything!"
"We'll start the first week school's out."
"Sounds great."

Such invitations hold excitement for me: excitement about the inquiry, about working collaboratively with others—listening, thinking, storying past experiences and teasing out new meaning. And so, in July 1991, a group of five women came together. In the safety and comfort of various living rooms we told stories from our practice, attempting to understand the different places in which we worked. We jointly created, over time, a new language to describe our collective experiences. We teased out the notion of competing stories in which teachers attempt to live out their teaching in new ways, ways suggesting a new paradigm.

In this chapter I present a competing story of teacher education, one that differs from the *familiar traditional* programs enacted in schools of education. This story was lived out by a young student teacher, Benita Dalton, as she engaged in the final two years of her teacher education program at the University of Calgary. I also raise the issue of inherent moral obligations when competing stories are nurtured and lived out within our institutions.

My relationship with Benita began in August 1989. She was entering her third year of university, a year in which she undertook her practicum. She had enrolled in the alternative program, an experimental program allowing her to participate in a sustained teaching experience over an eight-month period. I was her cooperating teacher. I was interested in exploring new possibilities in working more collaboratively with student teachers and university teachers. Together we lived a very different story of teacher education, a story of collaboration, reconstructed from journal entries and taped conversations spanning the two-year period from August 1989 to July 1991.

THE ALTERNATIVE PROGRAM: FORMING A RELATIONSHIP

Right from the start, Benita began to write in her journal about her experience in our grade-3 classroom. She wrote her observations of the first three days in school when teachers in shorts and sandals shared stories of summer vacation and negotiated timetables and subject preferences. She wrote of the first days for the children. I began to respond to her writing in the margins of her journal, as did Pat Hogan, her university teacher. Our three-way conversation placed us in close relationship over the months that followed.

As Benita wrote about her teaching, she generated important questions and wonders for herself. Her journal became the catalyst for a collaborative script forming the basis of our shared inquiry. She grappled with issues grounded in practice, became aware of the rhythms and cycles of a school year, and developed a capacity for self-evaluation. She found her voice and her place in her university and school settings. In reflecting on her third-year experience Benita spoke of feeling "a real sense of collaboration and what collaboration meant. The talking, the figuring out, the exchanging of ideas, the help, the openness" (Conversation, February 7, 1991).

These patterns of relating allowed her to live a new story of teacher education with new moral horizons established within our collaborative process. A further sense of collaboration came halfway through her practicum when her original university assignments were renegotiated to reflect the need to situate them more fully within the experience of each student teacher, cooperating teacher, and classroom. Benita was able to structure her own classroom-based inquiries and to allocate a percentage of marks to each piece of work. She wrote papers that fulfilled the requirements of her methods courses in language arts, math, social studies, and science. Her university teachers graded the work according to her suggested weighting of marks. In this way Benita was permitted to explore her own issues. Her inquiries, situated in practice, were grounded in real rather than hypothetical situations. This allowed her to take ownership of her learning. She explained:

> The university professors got a chance to see what we were doing in the classrooms and also because we were doing it, it was our

> own. . . trust was a big thing. Most students face the university bureaucracy and it's like "Well, we have to do it the university's way." But these people [the university teachers] were willing to take a chance. . . . They were willing to trust in us. (Conversation, February 7, 1991)

Benita recognized the connection between risk and trust. This feeling of trust made way for an increased moral obligation on her part. She worked to the very best of her ability. She did not want to let her teachers down. Her response made visible a new moral horizon called forth by the collaborative endeavor. She recalled:

> I think we definitely took more of a sense of pride in what we were doing. And knowing that they were there, they were supportive, they were our backbone. . . . Regular university is not like that . . . we were more equals and peers and that really helped. (Conversation, February 7, 1991)

To be more equal is to live a new story of teacher education, a competing story in sharp contrast with the sacred theory-practice story in which hierarchical relationships are defined and understood. The closeness of the collaborative relationship that Benita described allowed far more to be accomplished. Reciprocal acts of caring thus shaped her professional knowledge landscape and awakened her to new possibilities in teacher education. With this knowledge she entered the fourth and final year of her program.

RETURNING TO THE SACRED STORY: OUR RELATIONSHIP CONTINUED

During her fourth year, Benita continued to write a journal. I too documented my experience with a new group of grade-3 youngsters. Each of us responded to the other's journal, continuing our collaborative relationship. At the end of that year we talked at length about Benita's experience. It had not been an easy year. After a year spent constructing knowledge in collaboration with others, Benita found it difficult to adjust to the traditional style of her fourth-year university teachers. She found she was less able to voice her knowing. As well, she had difficulty connecting her knowledge from practice with teaching models presented in curriculum and instruction courses.

She had begun her year full of enthusiasm, believing that gaining more knowledge of theory would deepen and increase her understanding. She was willing to return to the sacred story of theory being passed down the conduit by university experts with knowledge of research in curriculum areas. Eager for this kind of knowledge, she spoke of her initial hopes:

> I was hoping that these courses would give me . . . new knowledge to tie in with my background knowledge and my experience with the classroom. . . . I guess I wanted knowledge that I didn't have. (Conversation, June 20, 1991)

Her frustration grew when the knowledge she was anticipating did not materialize. She wrote about her language arts class: "We seem to do a lot of activities, but I struggle with the question of where this fits in the classroom . . . these activities contain no meaning or foundation for me" (Journal Entry, September 25, 1990). Benita encountered activities stripped from the inquiries that produced them and stripped from their contexts. In the absence of context she was unable to make connections, connections that would allow her to feel confident as a first-year teacher. She explained:

> I was frustrated because it wasn't meaningful. If I was to put this activity into my program and my principal came in and said, "Why do you do this?" "I do this in language arts methods class!" It just doesn't cut it! It doesn't work! In a sense, I could see doing something better. (Conversation, June 20, 1991)

As she voiced her knowledge, Benita engaged in moral reflection that questioned the sacred story of the dissemination of knowledge by her university teachers. Awakening to her sense of knowing she saw the possibility for her own decision making—moral decision making—that could engage her in her own constructions rather than acting as an agent of received knowing. Benita's words represent a challenge to the status quo. Her feelings reflect a shift—a return to the competing story of teaching she experienced in the alternative program. Benita's knowledge, however, could be expressed only within the safety of relationships formed during the alternative program. In her university classes Benita remained silent, trapped in the traditional plot line.

Another of her journal entries triggered conversation. She wrote, "Even though I taught language arts last year, I couldn't relate my experience to this university class" (Journal Entry, September 25, 1990).

As we talked, Benita gave an example of the model of Writer's Workshop (Graves, 1983) presented by her university teacher:

> We always got the Reader's Digest version. Donald Graves in half a page, no justification why it is, just the five stages. Okay this is Donald Graves' Workshop but so what! Why does he say we should do this? There was nothing like that and I guess that's why it just didn't have any meaning . . . in practice everything dealt with meaning. (Conversation, June 20, 1991)

For Benita the rhetoric of conclusions dispensed in her methods class did not help her to understand the theory-practice relationship. But as we talked I storied for her my ongoing classroom adaptations of the Graves model over the previous four years. In this way Benita began to see my practice as a continuous reconstruction of Graves' initial theories. She understood my changing practice and this helped her make sense of her dilemma. She voiced a new understanding:

> That is what university doesn't tell us. They say, this is the model . . . but they don't say we can change it, so everyone of us who has taken a language methods course, who has never taught their own classroom . . . will go out to a classroom and do . . . Writer's Workshop step by step and I guess that's fine. You've got to go through it on your own . . . and then you can say, "Well it doesn't work this way, I have got to change it," but university doesn't tell you you can change it. . . . They don't say, this may not work! I guess that is the personal part that comes with practice that the university lacks. (Conversation, June 20, 1991)

With this understanding Benita could see the possibility of authoring her text as a constructivist teacher. Once again her moral horizon was reset in the context of shared stories. She was able to articulate a newfound sense of personal authority. In conversation she was able to connect theory with practice.

But the environment of her fourth-year university classes did not support the particular style of interactive learning she had come to value. Benita made the following comparison in her journal:

> There was a lot of talk and lengthy conversations about important stuff during my practicum year. I struggled in my journal for the answers to endless questions and people helped me . . . this year is not like that. The university does not provide that type of atmo-

> sphere. There you are, on your own, isolated. Sure you may ask questions, but they may never be answered. (Journal Entry, December 30, 1990)

Unable to experience relationship, unable to feel heard, Benita withdrew in relative silence. Her silence marked her return to the sacred story and to the behavior expected of her in this particular place on the professional knowledge landscape. But there was a cost to Benita, a cost she expressed in terms of her loss of self. She explained:

> I felt worthless again . . . I gained voice in practicum, a lot of voice and that voice made me feel very confident. But I get back to a situation where my voice isn't welcome . . . I definitely became voiceless again. . . . It was the idea of playing is this what the professor really wants to hear? It got back to playing that game again. (Conversation, June 20, 1991)

In the absence of collaboration, Benita experienced a sense of dislocation. Trapped in the old story she could only mourn the loss of what she had once known and valued. She wrote: "I have discovered the importance of talk. It reinforces what is being read or in essence learned. I need to have this and it is lacking in the class" (Journal Entry, December 17, 1990). Reflecting on this journal entry at the end of the year allowed Benita to envision the possibility of reclaiming what had been lost. She expressed her desire to be in relationship—to be in conversation with a team partner in her first year of practice:

> Without that dialogue, what I know may not be reinforced . . . that's how it works and how I've discovered it has worked for me. And that is why I think teaming is very important to me, especially in my first year. And I guess in practicum, the dialogue was always open, it was always there . . . I think that is why my practicum set us at a different level . . . we were always searching for the whys. (Conversation, June 20, 1991)

Voicing her feelings allowed Benita to retell the story she was intent on living out as she entered her first year of teaching, a story based on inquiry. She was unwilling to live a story of received knowing. She explained her thoughts:

> I almost get the feeling sometimes that the university wants to open our heads and fill them up with stuff. Maybe this is why so

> many teachers use models created by others without really understanding them. The university teaches that way, so do the teachers . . . this year because my story was very insignificant to the university picture . . . and because my head is being filled with these things that have no meaning or context, I can't fit them into my story, so therefore, I'm going to do it my way whether these fit or not. (Conversation, June 20, 1991)

Benita set her moral horizon. She recognized that she needed to construct and reconstruct her own knowledge to become the connected teacher she wanted to be (Belenky, Clinchy, Goldberger, & Tarule, 1986). Her fourth year was a chapter lived in opposition to the ongoing text she imagined writing for herself. Her sustained relationships, which supported her initial awakening as a teacher, allowed her to feel safe, safe enough to pursue her own way of teaching.

> I don't want to be the teachers I had when I went to school . . . I always want to be better. I always want to work at what I do. If something doesn't work, I want to change it and make it work. This comes probably from my home environment . . . from when I was a child—kind of like the Cinderella story. Cinderella always had to work . . . [laughing] so I guess that's where it comes from. . . . and I really find that getting to know the kids comes from my own sense of when I was little. I always was kind of silent so I think that if I had a teacher to draw me out I would have done better. I see myself as a caring trusting person . . . an observer—and not a criticizer—an encourager . . . I guess I want the children to see me as a person, not just as a teacher. (Conversation, July 19, 1991)

Benita's narrative draws attention to her deeply held moral work ethic as well as to her experience of emerging from silence. In the safety of relationships, Benita escaped from silence. Her experiences form models (Heilbrun, 1988) for her future relationships with children. For the children to see her as a person is to live a different story of teaching. In this way the stories Benita has lived and told frame her moral horizons. To live a competing story, to risk change, constitutes taking a giant step.

ANTICIPATING A COVER STORY AS A FIRST-YEAR TEACHER

At the June 1991 Convocation of the University of Calgary, Benita received her B.Ed. degree. She held in her hands a public symbol of conferred competence—her rite of passage into teaching. This certificate proved her mastery of an accepted body of knowledge; it embodied therefore the sacred story of the recipient as one holding knowledge. But as Benita and I talked in the weeks that followed, she spoke anxiously about not knowing enough. I began to see the conferring of her degree as a kind of mythology—a powerful mythology that would cause her to live a cover story of competence in her first year as a teacher. The cover story would mask her uncertainties. While Benita spoke of her fears openly and honestly in the safety of my living room, she told me she would not talk in this way with her school staff—administrators in particular. She knew it was important, in the face of the evaluation of her teaching, to live a story more closely resembling certainty rather than one that exposed uncertainties. To do that she would mentally edit her comments, taking care that she spoke of her days at school as being "just fine." She knew she could take her questions to the safety of trusted relationships, questions like:

> How do you know where to start? I'm not so much stuck with the physical setting. Getting in there setting your classroom doesn't scare me, but when those little kids come in the door, when those little people walk in that room, that scares me! . . . and I'm sure I will do fine when I come down to dealing with it . . . I guess it is establishing your rules, establishing a routine and beginning to build a trust system. . . . It is actually to get the ball rolling. (Conversation, June 20, 1991)

Benita's anxiety comes in part from the fact that so much of our teaching involves situational decision making and this kind of knowing cannot be conferred by educational institutions. For Benita, as for many teachers, beginnings are times of uncertainty. Such uncertainty is likely to be voiced only within safe places on the landscape. She explained:

> As a first-year teacher, what do you really know? . . . I have lots of ideas and sure I get the ideas from other teachers I worked with, I have ideas from . . . this year, but I haven't been able to practice. I don't know how they work . . . I guess it is coming down to knowing it. The principal wants to know the exact activity. You have got to know! I guess it is because . . . as a new teacher I'll be watched. At least that's my sense of it. It may not be a harmful eye either, but it will be there. (Conversation, June 20, 1991)

Benita's uncertainty will probably remain hidden from her new colleagues until trust is established. As well, her principal will be placed in a position of observing her cover story.

As she imagined her first teaching position, a cover story emerged relating to planning. She talked about using a journal rather than a traditional plan book. She explained how her timetable would act as a cover story:

> I think the underpinnings of my planning will be in a journal. It won't actually say "Today we will do this." It will be the figuring out of what actually goes on in my class. . . . I can see myself sort of playing the pleasing role, like having the timetable and such . . . but I'll develop an understanding of time and rhythm and how long it really takes something to occur and the importance of staying with it versus having rigid time slots. (Conversation, July 3, 1991)

Benita's planning will not resemble a regular day plan. Instead, her written journal entries will be an exploration of possible next steps in order to provide meaningful experiences for children. Her sense of teaching as inquiry will be embodied in her writing. This competing story of planning, honed in her practicum year, will form the basis of her daily decision making. Her decisions regarding relevant activities will be subsequently recorded. The events of the day will be thoughtfully orchestrated in order to nurture learning opportunities in an unhurried environment. In this way she will pay little heed to the rigid time slots represented on her timetable. Her timetable as a cover story creates a moral dilemma akin to the white lie. It represents game-playing as a response to demands via the conduit. Her lesson plans will be responsive to the particular children in her care. She explains her competing story of planning:

> The people who took the regular practicum made tons of lesson plans. They could write you up a lesson plan that had objectives and motivational activities and anticipatory sets. . . . I struggled with that a long time and basically I just figured it out by myself. . . . I guess I just take multiple resources and I amalgamate them and create something. It doesn't come from an activity book . . . I really seek to understand the material. That's something that's very important to me. I think people in the regular practicum have learned to get their activities from books . . . separate from a classroom of children. (Conversation, July 5, 1991)

Benita does not subscribe to the accountability embodied in technical-rational models of instruction for generic groups of children. Instead she adopts the role of a curriculum maker (Clandinin & Connelly, 1992) as she demonstrates her capacity for inquiry and her willingness to pursue wisdom. Benita's plans embody relationship, connectedness, and the desire for more authentic communication with children. To work in this way is a moral achievement. Benita can be responsive to children and to the mandated curriculum as she lives out her competing story. She can find freedom as a curriculum maker within the boundaries established by the department of education. While her long-range planning will fall within an acceptable range of practice, she explains the need to live a cover story in daily planning:

> The sense of long-range plans is important . . . because it will give me a sense of how long I have to cover something. I'll think of the whole year, but I'll think of it in chunks . . . by looking at the curriculum. . . . I would construct the long-range plan . . . if they want the actual day-to-day lesson plan, I'm in trouble maybe. You know, and maybe that's a game I'll have to play. I'll have to wait and see. . . . I guess that's something I need to figure out as a teacher on that staff. (Conversation, July 5, 1991)

Benita is aware of the element of situational decision making that will be called forth depending on her placement. She is prepared to live a cover story that will allow her to be true to her own moral horizons. This awareness will help her to avoid turning her competing story into a conflicting one that might prove detrimental to her. As she lives her cover story, some of her knowledge will remain hidden. We talked further about the stresses for first-year teachers. Benita explained:

> [laughing] Everything is going to cause stress . . . the parent who opposes your program . . . and doesn't believe that whole language is the way children should be taught . . . do I have enough confidence in my program to defend it properly . . . the stress of "Am I doing a good job?" . . . the stress I put upon myself. . . . "Are these kids learning something? Am I getting to them?" . . . the stress of how long 'til Christmas . . . the stress of beginning. (Conversation, July 5, 1991)

While Benita could laugh with me about potential stress, the fact that she named her fears is cause for reflection. Her fears are closely connected to the moral horizons she sets, moral horizons reflecting her commitment to children and to the practice of teaching.

VOICING COMPETING STORIES: MORAL IMPLICATIONS

There were times when Benita did not or could not live out a cover story. She spoke from the heart in job-interview situations, not realizing that the views she expressed were outside the range of answers expected by her interviewers. She gave an example:

> The principal asked me something about consequences regarding disciplining children. . . and I said, "That depends, it depends on the story, it depends on the child. . . . I'm not going to be judgmental I guess . . . I am there to listen . . . I have empathy for the child . . . you still discipline but you just do it in a gentle manner. One that's not going to hurt or hurt him more I guess is a good way to put it . . . to let him know that you're there—that you still think that he's a good person . . . that you want to help him with his problem." (Conversation, July 5, 1991)

Benita's stance on discipline had everything to do with the theme of caring and fidelity to relationships (Noddings, 1984) she had been introduced to in the alternative program. Understanding the child's story was crucial. But Benita sensed that speaking a language of consequences was an expectation of those conducting job interviews. She was concerned that her view of teaching and thinking about discipline would neither be understood nor rewarded by those positioned higher in the conduit. She believed she could be seen as weak when she did not speak the language of a moral technician spelling out consequences for misdemeanors. Unable to live a rhetoric of conclusions, Benita set her moral horizon based on her commitment to children. Those of us who had nurtured Benita's competing story suddenly became aware of a moral dilemma. Had we placed at risk those student teachers who chose to work collaboratively with us? Had we given those beginning teachers the language of a new paradigm that would place them outside the boundaries of the dominant story? I thought about the language Benita used to express her goals. It could be unwise for her to say things such as "one of my goals is for each child who comes into my classroom to like to be there." (Conversation, June 26, 1991) and "you have to listen to the children and let them tell you their story before you can begin the day" (Conversation, July 3, 1991).

Benita's voice uses the language of the mother tongue (LeGuin, 1989), the language of the feminine that values listening. Listening to children presents a very different view of teaching; it is a catalyst for collaboration and inquiry into learning and teaching. But is this mother tongue outside the range of acceptable practice? Does Benita know the range? The ground is tricky. There is a need for first-year teachers to keep their ears to the ground in order to speak a language within the boundaries of the sacred story.

By maintaining a relationship with Benita, I know I can help her to better understand the politics of meshing her competing story of teaching with the sacred story. She in turn will help me to sustain the courage to create new possibilities in my teaching. Within safe places, all of us can remain open to change. It is as Benita says:

> At one point in just going to university I figured you got to a point and you knew, but I think now there are just too many changing variables: students change, curriculum changes, school changes, you change. (Conversation, June 26, 1991)

Benita is poised to live a competing story of teaching by choice. It is refreshing to see a young woman willing to think reflectively about the total pattern of education to which she is committed. She is willing to live with the uncertainty and the inevitable change that mark education as constructive achievement (Dewey, 1900).

CHAPTER 6

Teacher Education in the Conduit: Competing Stories

D. Jean Clandinin and F. Michael Connelly

In this chapter we want to think through the ways Chapters 4 and 5 build on and add to the ideas of Chapters 1 through 3. Chapters 1 through 3 developed the idea of a professional knowledge landscape as the context for teachers' personal practical knowledge. We imagined the landscape as a professional location that teachers experienced as filled with epistemological and moral dilemmas. As we imagined it, the landscape was composed of two places, in-classroom and out-of-classroom places. We characterized these two places as being different. The classroom place on the landscape is a place of teaching activity and interwoven stories of these activities. The out-of-classroom place on the landscape is one of abstract talk about abstract policies and prescriptions. These abstract policies and prescriptions are fed into the landscape via a conduit that connects the world of theory with the world of practice. Dilemmas are created as teachers move back and forth between the two places on the landscape.

Chapter 3 expanded this notion by sketching a historical development of the professional knowledge landscape. Craig's account of one of her students, Carla, and a discussion of Marion Connelly's early-in-the-century teaching experience, were used to build links between the professional landscape of schools and the personal knowledge landscape out of schools.

Chapters 3 through 5 pointed to places off the professional knowledge landscape. Chapter 3 pointed to the personal and focused on a matrix of relationships between the personal and the professional landscapes. Chapters 4 and 5 are focused on the site of teacher education located somewhere in the conduit between the university and the professional knowledge landscape of schools. The two chapters were written around the preservice teacher education experiences of two teachers,

Sonia and Benita, who were part of an alternative teacher education program. Sonia and Benita spent part of their time in a normal teacher education program and part of their time in this alternative program. Specifically, the alternative program consisted of the third year in a four-year program. It was, therefore, preceded by two years of a normal program and followed by one year of a normal program.

TEACHER EDUCATION IN THE CONDUIT?

The discussion in Chapter 1 of the conduit named the university as one of the places where abstract, morally oriented material is prepared and funneled into schools. As teacher education programs are normally conceived, the main story that holds them together is one of student teachers being taught skills and knowledge (both liberal and professional), methodologies for using the skills and teaching the knowledge, and practice in the application of these skills and knowledge to teaching. This story has been named, elaborated, and widely discussed in recent years by philosophers (e.g., Oakeshott, 1962; Schön, 1983, 1991) and educators (e.g., Russell & Munby, 1992). They call it "technical rationalism." It is a form of rationalism because ideas and those who know (university teachers) are given dominant positions over those who do (school practitioners). Knowing is preeminent over doing. Better doing comes from more and better knowing. And it is "technical" because there is a presumed technology by which it is assumed that the university knowers get the school doers to do what the knowers know they should. This general story of teacher education is common, says Schön (1983), to most of the professions. In differing ways, and with different subject matter, the plot line for all the professions tends to follow the technical-rational outline. And this plot, more generally, is set up by the plot of the sacred theory-practice story described in Chapter 1. In effect, teacher education programs are embedded in the overall plot line of the sacred story.

As students proceed through teacher education programs, they progress from university to school. Though not in a tight lockstep series, they tend to be passed down the conduit from liberal arts and science professors to foundations of education professors to methods professors to cooperating teachers. Each step of the way owes its validity to the step before it and is seen as a prerequisite to the step after it. Knowledge of the disciplines is thought to be prerequisite to teaching the disciplines; understanding the history of education and the psychology and sociology of learning is thought to be prerequisite to studying the methods of teaching; and studying the methods of teaching is thought to be prerequisite to practicing teaching.

And what is practicing teaching thought to be? Basically, it is thought to be practicing the various levels of theory experienced in the conduit. So much is this the case that new teachers who do well in practice teaching are commonly thought to bring "young blood" for rejuvenating the profession, or they are resented for bringing unneeded, perhaps disruptive, new ideas. And these ideas are nurtured by theoreticians even on the professional knowledge landscape. Returning to the conduit metaphor, university faculty or their representatives step onto the in-classroom professional knowledge landscape along with their student teacher protegés, whom they supervise, and evaluate how well their students apply theoretical knowledge and skills. Anything genuine or "real," such as problems with children, budget shortages, teacher transfer, collapsing of departments and whatnot, is considered too concrete and not essential to the practice-teaching task. Student teachers inevitably are visitors screened from ongoing life on the professional knowledge landscape. Their sense of themselves is not primarily that of professionals but, rather, that of people learning to demonstrate their applied theory capability. It is Sonia and Benita's stories, told in the preceding two chapters, of being in an alternative program that allows us to show the influence of this part of the sacred story in teacher education.

COMPETING STORIES OF TEACHER EDUCATION IN THE CONDUIT

In the following two sections, we argue that both the alternative program and the normal program are situated in the conduit. The alternative program was designed to be a competing story of teacher education, but it was not designed to be lived out outside the conduit. We retell Sonia's and Benita's stories from Chapters 4 and 5 to make this clear.

Let us begin with Sonia. She was a parent who worked in her children's school as a parent volunteer. As a parent volunteer she was comfortable in both the in-classroom and out-of-classroom places on the professional knowledge landscape. In addition, she had been a noncertified teacher in an after-school languages program. Encouraged by the teacher with whom she had been a parent volunteer, she entered a teacher education program. By the time she had completed the four-year program, the confidence she had felt as a parent volunteer had evaporated. In other words, she began her teacher education program feeling comfortable and confident on the professional knowledge landscape and ended her program much more confused about the stories she would live on it. How could this have happened? We first try to understand this unexpected outcome in terms of stories of teacher education within the conduit.

Two years before Clandinin met Sonia in the third-year alternative program, Sonia had entered a regular four-year teacher education program on the advice of Jude, the teacher with whom Sonia had been a parent volunteer. Jude, meanwhile, was completing her master's degree with Clandinin on a part-time basis and was on the steering committee of the alternative program. We have already pointed out that Sonia was comfortable and confident on the professional knowledge landscape. But this confidence was not primarily professional confidence because Sonia was positioned on the landscape as a parent volunteer. In fact, she questioned whether she would make a good teacher. It was Jude, and the parents of the students Sonia taught in the language program who knew her work, who eventually convinced her that she could translate what she was doing into the professional role of a teacher. Though her ups and downs are not documented in the chapter, she did gain professional confidence over the first two years of the normal program. When Clandinin met her she was earning good grades. When she left the regular story of teacher education experienced in the first two years of her program and joined the competing story in the alternative third-year program, again at Jude's encouragement and at the prospect of being able to work with Jude as her cooperating teacher, she did not have a strong sense of how different this alternative program was. She had little sense that it was an alternative story to the sacred story of teacher education. The way Sonia lived and told her story in the third year suggested that she was still living out the plot lines for a successful student that had led to her academic success through the first two years of her program (concrete documentation of this particular point is found in Clandinin et al., 1993, pp. 197–198).

Sonia struggled with the plot line of the story in which the alternative program was embedded. However, she experienced success and was highly rated by those with whom she worked. This brings us up to the time of the material presented in Chapter 4, which was collected and written around the fourth year of her program in which she returned to the regular teacher education story. From the vantage point of being a student in the normal program, Sonia looked back to her experience of the alternative teacher education program. In addition to being a student, she served as a teacher aide working with Josh, a student in difficulty.

One set of stories Sonia told related to her experience of writing course papers. An emphasis in the alternative program had been to put practice before theory. Consequently, course papers had their starting point in the classroom experiences of the student teachers. Sonia tried to carry this forward into her fourth year, and was initially encouraged to do so by her fourth-year program professors. In practice, however, as shown in Chapter 4, doing so did not prove satisfactory and she found herself penalized when she did not follow certain expected ways of doing things. On this point, after citing discussions with a professor, she said, "There must be a certain way to do this." By the end of the term, she said she had gone back to writing in the ways expected by the regular teacher education story.

Another set of stories revolved around Sonia's decision to take an additional mathematics course. She said she began her fourth year realizing that "maybe I do know a few things that I need to know to become a teacher." But, by midway through the year, she enrolled in an extra mathematics course as her "last chance to learn enough to teach." In effect, the sacred theory-practice story reasserted its grip on Sonia. She again felt that knowledge of teaching must be given to her by the university. She began her four-year program thinking that "I was going to go and after I left, I would know everything I would need to know as a teacher." But near the end of the program she said that she "still needed to know more."

Sonia left her teacher education program still waiting to become filled with knowledge from the conduit. The irony in this is that there is a kind of double jeopardy offered by the conduit. On the one hand, it has a sense of certainty and a definable set of things to be learned by preservice teachers. On the other hand, student teachers are taught that they will never know as much as their university professors. There are always more and more advanced courses to take. Furthermore, student teachers are taught by their university professors that there is a knowledge explosion of which their professors are a part. Teachers begin teaching having been taught they have incomplete knowledge. In this view, they need to continue to learn through returning to the university for professional development.

The retelling of Benita's story has many of the same marks as Sonia's. Benita also came to the alternative program after two years in the normal teacher education program. She, however, did not have Sonia's background experience as a parent volunteer on the in- and out-of-classroom professional knowledge landscape. While Sonia academically adapted quickly to the first two years of the normal teacher education program, Benita did not. Accordingly, she came to the alternative program already living and telling a story of teacher education that was somewhat different from the one Sonia lived and told. Benita came to the program because she saw it as learning how to teach in an alternative way. Sonia was there primarily because of her association with Jude.

Though Benita eagerly chose the alternative program for the possibility it might offer, there were indications that her previous experience in the normal teacher education program made her suspicious of some of the activities and purposes of the new program. For example, one of the first assignments was to keep a reflective journal. Benita was initially reluctant to write about how she was making sense of her experience. In her earlier experiences of journal writing at the university, she had been assigned a specific task for her journal. The more open-ended journal assignment in the alternative program left her feeling uncomfortable because she "didn't know what we were supposed to write." This reluctance is easily understood in terms of her personal educational biography played out in the context of the normal teacher education program embedded in the sacred theory-practice story. However, Benita quickly adapted to the new plot line and, as is evident in Chapter 5, she not only found the program very much to her liking but was also able to articulate in writing and in conversation what the program meant for her and why it was different from the normal program.

As with Sonia in Chapter 4, Chapter 5 picks up Benita's story line during the fourth year of the program, when she returned to the normal teacher education program. Whereas Sonia continued to struggle with issues of competence and what was expected of her, Benita withdrew in relative silence, saying "It was the idea of playing 'is this what the professor wants to hear?'" Sonia and Benita responded in very different ways to the competing stories of teacher education in the conduit. Sonia struggled to live both stories, eventually succumbing to the sacred story; Benita held to the story of the alternative program and lived a cover story in the fourth year of the normal program. At the end of Chapter 5, in conversations that took place after the completion of her fourth year, Benita looked forward to her teaching, recognizing that she would need to tell a cover story to be successful in the out-of-classroom place on the professional knowledge landscape. As Davies tells Benita's story, Benita knew it was important, in the face of the evaluation of her teaching, to live a story more resembling certainty, rather than one that exposed uncertainties. It is clear that Benita sensed what we believe to be the case, namely, that there is a continuity between the story that she lived out in the normal teacher education program and the story she will need to live out on the out-of-classroom place on the professional knowledge landscape.

Both the out-of-classroom place on the professional knowledge landscape and the normal teacher education program are greatly influenced by the conduit. It may be that alternative programs of teacher education that attempt to become competing stories but that remain in the conduit are also greatly influenced by it. We say more about that later but first we turn our attention to preservice teacher education outside the conduit.

PRESERVICE TEACHER EDUCATION OUTSIDE THE CONDUIT

Our retelling of Sonia's story above missed an important part of her preservice story told in Chapter 4. This is a story of her work with a special-needs student, Josh. Her work with Josh turned out to be an important part of her teacher education even though it did not take place in the conduit and was not, therefore, planned for or assessed in conduit terms. The story prescribed for Sonia to live out with Josh was, however, prescribed by the sacred theory-practice story. Even though her work with Josh was outside the teacher education program, the story governing her relationship with Josh was determined by the conduit, which specified ways in which special education children were to be treated. Josh was a child who, according to the conduit, fit into a segregated educational setting. Because no setting was immediately available, Sonia was hired to work with Josh in his regular classroom. The story that Sonia and Josh lived together allowed Josh to begin to feel confident enough to fit into the regular grade-1 classroom. Even though he was increasingly able to fit into the classroom, the special education story for Josh was still in place. Sonia did not try to prevent his placement in the segregated program when the space became available. By not speaking up she felt responsible for what she considered to be a wrong decision. She attributed her own inaction on his behalf to her lack of confidence, a confidence she had expected to be given to her by the conduit. She said, "It bugs me . . . because one little kid got screwed around because I am waiting to get this confidence up."

What we see in this story of Sonia and Josh is that Sonia is beginning to recognize that the sacred story is not a story that would help her live out her teaching. She acted in one way within the classroom but lacked the confidence to carry it forward in the out-of-classroom setting where she might have intervened with decision makers responsible for Josh's future. Because she could not speak the language of the conduit with authority, she silenced herself. In this we see the dilemma of Chapter 1. As Sonia moved back and forth between her classroom and out-of-classroom places on the landscape, she experienced the dilemma teachers experience as they move across a boundary separating markedly different epistemological and moral parts of the landscape. And we also see her growing sense of doubt about the efficacy of the sacred story embedded in the teacher education program—a story that she had been fully anticipating from the time she entered the four-year program. Another point worth noting here is that her professional knowledge, her sense of herself as a professional, is fostered more deliberately and more directly in keeping with that of other teachers by her experience of teacher education outside the conduit than it was by her teacher education program itself. She learned more about the professional knowledge dilemmas of teaching in this out-of-conduit, out-of-program, experience with Josh than she could have learned in her four formal years of teacher education.

THE POSSIBILITY OF CONSTRUCTING COMPETING STORIES OF TEACHER EDUCATION IN THE CONDUIT

Positioning an alternative story of teacher education within the conduit means that extended negotiations are needed to keep it alive and to continually evolve new aspects of the plot. Furthermore, these aspects of a new plot must be worked out by universities, teacher associations, boards, government, and other groups that are authorized by the sacred story to prepare and funnel things down the conduit. However, this set of negotiations would result only in a slightly altered version of the regular story of teacher education. In addition, there must be continual negotiation of the plot line with teachers, principals, student teachers, children, parents, and others in both places on the professional knowledge landscape. This means that it is not enough for a creative and ambitious university faculty group to negotiate a new plot line for teacher education with their dean and faculty colleagues; they must also negotiate at the other end of the conduit and continue to negotiate with those with whom they work in schools. There are now versions of alternative teacher education stories where the negotiation mostly occurs at the university. But these are essentially alternative programs experienced on the in- and out-of-classroom places on the professional knowledge landscape as a version of the sacred story.

The alternative program in which Sonia and Benita's stories are embedded was, in contrast, a program worked out primarily on the professional knowledge landscape. But this alternative program no longer exists. Why not? Our way of explaining this is that program participants, both university and school, did not acknowledge the positioning of the program within the conduit. In the short term, the program was protected from the influence of the conduit by thoughtful school principals and university administrators. But, in the long haul, the amount of energy needed to maintain the buffer could not be sustained.

The demise of the alternative program strikingly makes the point that it is not only that student teachers, schoolteachers, and university teachers are prisoners of their biographies. The sacred story in which teacher education programs are embedded is responsible for the difficulty of establishing and maintaining a new story of teacher education. An alternative program that genuinely creates an alternative story of teacher education runs afoul not only of participant biographies but also of the sacred story.

PART III

PROFESSIONAL KNOWLEDGE LANDSCAPES OF BEGINNING TEACHERS

CHAPTER 7

Coming to Know on the Professional Knowledge Landscape: Benita's First Year of Teaching

Cheryl Craig

In this chapter, I follow Benita Dalton from her teacher education program to her first year of teaching. In Chapters 5 and 6 Benita's experience in her third and fourth years of teacher education are discussed.

I came to know Benita in the summer of 1991 through our mutual acquaintances: Jean Clandinin, Annie Davies, and Pat Hogan. Jean was my doctoral thesis advisor and Annie, Pat, and I knew each other because we were teachers in the same school board.

When she graduated, Benita was hired as a substitute teacher by the same board. She taught in eight different schools during her first year of teaching. She served as a substitute teacher at Annie Davies's school, Riverview, about three and one-half days a week. Benita also worked as a clerk in a grocery store for about 16 hours per week.

This chapter features Benita's attempt as a beginning substitute teacher to secure a regular teaching position. As I trace the difficulties Benita encountered, her sense of herself as a good teacher comes to the fore. I follow the ways Benita comes to situate herself on the professional knowledge landscape by highlighting the tensions she experiences between her image of good teaching cultivated in the alternative program and notions of good teaching she encounters in the school system.

BENITA ENCOUNTERS COMPETING NOTIONS OF GOOD TEACHING

As Benita worked with numerous children in different schools, the children shared their beliefs about good teaching with her. The children assessed her work as a teacher against a kind of standard they had constructed of good teaching. Benita listened carefully to the students' talk, and was mindful of their situations. She explained the significance of her interactions with them by saying, "I constantly learn from the children. I think that children teach us and that is how we become 'good teachers.' We do so by listening carefully and by being empathetic" (Conversation, June 5, 1992).

What Benita was expressing in her first-year work with students was her image of teaching as personal relationships with students, an image she began to develop in her practicum year of her teacher education program. The image started to crystallize when she read *The Velveteen Rabbit* (Williams, 1981) with Annie Davies and her students. Benita saw herself as being like the beloved rabbit who became real when it was loved. As Benita developed loving relationships with students, she felt she became a "real teacher." Pat Hogan, one of her university teachers, assured Benita of her authenticity by saying, "You are real, Benita . . . I have been wanting to tell you that for a long time" (Journal Entry, March 3, 1992). Benita's experience of reading *The Velveteen Rabbit* with Annie and her class, accompanied by Pat's reassuring comments, stuck with Benita and a teaching image began to form.

But Benita as a substitute teacher found herself unable to develop satisfying relationships with students. Supervising students and living out other teachers' lesson plans did not resonate with Benita's image of good teaching. Neither did the idea of being a substitute, one who was not doing the real thing, sit well with her. Benita felt a dissonance between her substituting experiences and the image of good teaching she held. She felt cut off from students as a substitute teacher in much the same way as she felt cut off "from the real world" (Conversation, October 23, 1991) as a fourth-year education student in the professional knowledge landscape of the university. Benita felt she was again in situations that were "superficial, not real"; situations in which she also felt "superficial, not real" (Conversation, October 23, 1991).

Benita found it hard to be the kind of good teacher she wished to be when all she had were "little flashes" of teaching (Conversation, October 23, 1991). To Benita, supervising students in classrooms, something she often did as a substitute, was like "watching television all day" (Conversation, October 23, 1991). She missed the "action and interaction" (Conversation, October 23, 1991) of real teaching. Benita craved ownership experiences, experiences in which she could express more of her knowledge. Benita wanted to shape teaching situations; she did not want her teaching story to be shaped by others.

Benita doubted whether she could develop ownership in a substitute teaching position. She found it difficult to imagine herself living her good-teacher image as a substitute teacher. The good-teacher image she held collided with what was expected of her in certain schools. "Supervising kids" (Conversation, September 30, 1991), "feeling like a referee" (Conversation, October 8, 1991), "supervising book exchanges" (Conversation, November 2, 1991), and "jutting in and out of many classrooms" (Conversation, November 10, 1991) did not fit with her image of good teaching. Benita regretted "one shot days . . . not doing anything that was her own" (Conversation, November 10, 1991). She felt that ownership was a prerequisite for her to be a good teacher.

> I need ownership . . . I don't think I can get it from a substitute teaching position. It is like getting a snapshot, a frame from a movie, but I am never there for the whole movie. (Conversation, November 10, 1991)

Benita did not feel free to take ownership as a substitute teacher. On the contrary, she felt like "a figurine coming in and being there," a nonperson without voice, agency, or ownership (Journal Entry, October 23, 1991).

BENITA EXPRESSES HER GOOD-TEACHER IMAGE AS SHE PREPARES FOR JOB INTERVIEWS

In December, when Benita was scheduled for a job interview, she asked if we could do a practice interview. I agreed. My experience on hiring committees framed my interview questions. As might be expected, Benita's personal image of a good teacher emerged in her responses:

> *Cheryl:* Here is a question which is often asked in interviews. . . . What qualities do you see in yourself which make you a "good teacher"?
>
> *Benita:* . . . I'm an ongoing learner and a good listener. I am empathetic and innovative. I enjoy challenges . . . I'm innovative . . . I am always looking for new ways to do things. I am also reflective. . . . That is very important. . . . I think about how I am going to do something, I put it into action, and then I reevaluate it . . . I think about the variables, I listen to the kids, I question what does this mean, what does that mean. (Conversation, December 9, 1991)

In describing herself as a good teacher, Benita highlighted the importance of listening and responding to the students. She went on: "I think about the issues of teaching. I think about how I have grown as a teacher. These points are part of me being an ongoing learner" (Conversation, December 9, 1991). For a second time, Benita associated teacher growth with being a good teacher. Her response reminded me of earlier comments she had made about herself, particularly in October, when Benita handed me her third- and fourth-year teacher education journals to read. I was already holding her first-year teaching journal in my hand. Our conversation went this way:

> *Cheryl:* Benita, can you see changes in yourself from one journal to another?
> *Benita:* I really would not want to think about it as change . . . what I would call it is growth. (Conversation, October 29, 1991)

Feeling a sense of growth was an important part of Benita's knowledge of herself as a good teacher.

Benita also described how she would handle discipline in a classroom in the practice interview:

> Discipline? It is a collaborative effort. Discipline comes in understanding a child . . . the best way to understand what is going on is to talk with the child, have a dialogue and communicate with a child. But for me to blatantly discipline a child would be wrong. . . . It is important for me to listen to his story because everyone has their own story. Discipline is very situational; very individual. (Conversation, December 9, 1991)

Benita again associated good teaching with listening and expressed this knowledge in potential classroom discipline situations.

The points Benita highlighted in our December interview were similar to the points she made in a portfolio she prepared for employment purposes. In the portfolio, Benita extended her knowledge of reflective practice. She wrote,

> I see myself as a reflective practitioner. I am a person who wonders and questions. I think about daily happenings in my classroom: what is going on with my students, how I am making sense of being a teacher, and how I am figuring out the curriculum. (Portfolio Entry, June 5, 1992)

In the practice interview, Benita also revisited her idea of teacher growth and named journal writing as her way to chronicle it.

> I write in a journal to get my thoughts out and to reflect on my classroom practice. I write in a journal because it allows me to go back in time and read what I have written to see if I have come up with new insights and answers to my questions. My journal is a place where I can see how I have grown professionally. (Conversation, June 5, 1991)

Benita linked growth to her image of a good teacher.

UNDERSTANDING THE POLITICAL NATURE OF HIRING SITUATIONS

As Benita's good-teacher image found expression, multiple tensions arose between the image she expressed and her lack of success with job applications. Benita often stated: "I just wish the school system could see the qualities the children see in me" (Conversations, April 10, 1992; April 21, 1992). Benita sensed that her image of the good teacher did not fit with the institution's demands. If she were a good teacher, she reasoned, she would be teaching her own class, not working as a substitute teacher. Benita began to doubt her abilities as a teacher:

> Sometimes I feel sad and depressed because I hear a lot of good stuff about my work from children and fellow teachers. But it makes me wonder why I don't have a full-time job. I wonder if I am missing something? (Conversation, January 11, 1992)

Benita felt she had been recognized as a good teacher in the alternative program but was not recognized in the school system. While Benita received positive feedback from individual teachers and schools, this information was not available to hiring committees. And when she went for interviews, she was told she did a "good job" but no constructive comments were offered. Benita was unable to grasp a sense of the good teacher for which the school system was looking. She felt she could "only guess at the picture . . . they constructed of her as a teacher." Even though she listened carefully to the positive stories people were sharing with her, she sensed her knowing of other people's constructions of herself as a good teacher were at best a partial telling (Field notes, December 19, 1991). As she faced job uncertainty, Benita's inability to "get in the door of the school system" disappointed and frustrated her.

After an unsuccessful job interview, there was the next exchange:

Benita: It is like you wind yourself up, you prepare yourself for an interview, you anticipate you will be a teacher . . .
Cheryl: You start to build the story of your life around a job interview?
Benita: Yes, and then it is . . . like a drop; you just drop. . . . Like what is the magic you can reveal that an interview committee want to hear in twenty minutes? (Conversation, December 19, 1992)

Benita wanted to figure out the images of good teaching held by hiring committees so she could give them back in the next round of interviews. She reasoned that would be a way to get a job.

Benita's concerns were heightened when she realized that most of her peers already had jobs. This realization fueled Benita's uncertainties about herself as a good teacher:

> I lose faith in myself. People have advocated for me saying I am a "good teacher" but maybe other people are seeing something different. . . . Can they see deeper in my soul and see I am not a "good teacher"? (Conversation, June 25, 1992)

Benita also thought about what she could learn from the circumstances of her peers' hiring situations. It seemed to her that many of them had been in places where they had been noticed: male teachers in elementary schools, presenters of prominent presentations, placements in particular schools, and so on. Benita thought about how she could "market" herself, so she, too, could be a good teacher in a place where she would be noticed.

Benita also came to an uncomfortable understanding about how teachers get hired. She noted, "It is not what you know; it is who you know!" and realized that a good teacher could be assured work as much by networking as by an ability to do the job.

Benita prepared for another round of job applications by polishing her portfolio for distribution. She did not anticipate the nature of Annie's response to her draft portfolio. Annie told Benita that her portfolio would be "beautifully received" by her former university teachers but questioned whether the material would be understood by hiring committees. She wondered if Benita's portfolio would "suit her audience" (Conversation, June 5, 1992). Annie explained:

> So it is like you can be talking about teaching in whatever way you want but if the person you are doing it for is not receptive to the

> format it is not going to get you a job. . . . You have to be crystal clear so you are not misinterpreted. I mean I know this man you are taking your portfolio to and I do not know that he would know the kind of language you are trying to talk to him with. (Conversation, June 4, 1992)

Benita's image of the good teacher had been cultivated during her practicum experiences and would be understood by those who cultivated it. As Annie pointed out, Benita had constructed a portfolio with a former audience in mind, not a present audience. It would not fit—just as Benita's letter to a principal, in which she wrote "I am busy trying to figure out the teaching profession and my story as a teacher" (Letter, November 1, 1991) did not fit—with the certainty expected of beginning teachers. Annie advised Benita to cut "the philosophizing and tell them what you have done" (Conversation, June 4, 1992). Annie's response resonated with the words of a school principal who spoke to Benita's practicum class. Benita remembered the principal saying, "No philosophizing; just get down to the essentials!" (Conversation, October 29, 1991).

Annie told Benita she did not need to market herself as the good teacher as much as she needed to figure out what was relevant to the school system. Annie also tried to illustrate how educators intentionally give different expressions of their images of teaching and of themselves as good teachers for hiring and promotion purposes. She likened the process to a "game" (Conversation, June 4, 1992). Benita responded by saying, "I'm frustrated . . . I don't know what the game is. I'm just trying to get in!" (Conversation, June 4, 1992).

Job uncertainty was a frustration that had been welling up in Benita for over a year. Her physical exhaustion from working five back-to-back days in two different jobs, coupled with her frustration of not knowing where she would be working the following year, prompted her to say: "I'm driving myself crazy . . . I need some security . . . I just do not want to be substitute teaching next year . . . I've reached the point of frustration . . . I am very tired" (Conversation, June 4, 1992).

In response, Annie reminded Benita of Benita's life story, a story of "never having anything easy," a story of a life marked by obstacles, a lack of security, and a determination to overcome obstacles. Benita had lived her life so that it would be different from the lives of some of her family members. Benita's "better life" (Conversation, November 10, 1991) had been carefully authored. Having now to work as a substitute, one who is not real, after having carefully shaped herself to be a "real" teacher was deeply troubling to Benita.

Annie and I tried to give Benita back her story a second time, this time emphasizing our knowledge of how Benita had overcome difficulties and stressing our belief that she would be able to overcome this one. Benita joked, "It is about time . . . I deserve something easy!" (Conversation, June 4, 1992).

Annie thought our conversations with Benita helped her prepare for job interviews "in a more informed way" (Conversation, June 6, 1992). She felt Benita's knowing would be informed by the school system's way of knowing and by Benita's personal image of good teaching. What Annie and I had done was to share part of the game with Benita.

Benita seemed puzzled by our responses and by the change in our language but she came to understand that Annie and I were informing her of other constructions of the good teacher so she could get through the door. Benita learned she needed different expressions of good teaching in hiring situations before she would be hired.

CONNECTING BENITA'S IMAGE OF A GOOD TEACHER TO THE SACRED THEORY-PRACTICE STORY

Benita's knowledge of good teaching was not initially bounded by the sacred story of theory-practice. She expressed an image of good teaching that was cultivated in the alternative program, an against-the-grain approach to teacher education. The alternative program, for the school systems and for the university, was a competing story of how teacher education could be lived, a story that challenged the sacred theory-practice relationship. The alternative program questioned traditional roles and responsibilities of the university and the school system and the relationship between the two institutions. Furthermore, the program put Benita in association with people who might be storied as being on the margins of their professional groups. Jean Clandinin, for example, could be storied as being on the edge of the education faculty because she was searching for alternate ways to live the story of university teacher as expert. Pat Hogan found herself on the margins of the university community because she was an outsider, a secondment, someone on loan from the school system. Pat's desire to participate in living and telling a competing story of teacher education challenged the part she was to play in the sacred story for which she was on loan from the school board. Pat and Annie could also be storied as being on the edge of their practice community due in part to their involvement with teacher research projects and collaborative research with Jean. The same could be said for me. Like those of Annie and Pat, my story did not fit within traditional stories in either the university or the school system. These competing stories were part of the professional knowledge landscape in which Benita was being educated. Benita was being cultivated by people who were imagining ways of changing the sacred story. And Benita repeatedly expressed her personal practical knowledge cultivated within this competing story in her interactions with school and school board personnel. Benita, a promising young teacher articulating a competing image of good teaching, began to doubt her abilities. In blaming herself, Benita gave a gendered response.

Her adherence to the competing story is the story of this chapter. It is a story told around interviews, job applications, and portfolios that contribute to her awakening to the discrepancy between this story and the sacred theory-practice story as it is expressed by hiring committees. Through consultation with friends/colleagues she learns the value of cover stories, which have the potential to allow her to hold on to her image of a good teacher nurtured in the competing story of teacher education while, at the same time, expressing an image of a good teacher compatible with the sacred theory-practice story that has the potential to secure her a job.

AFTERWORD

In the 1993–1994 school year, Benita was given a temporary contract to fill in for a teacher on maternity leave at Riverview School. Benita has recently received a letter informing her there will be no regular teaching positions available in the 1994–1995 school year.

CHAPTER 8

A Story of Tim's Coming to Know Sacred Stories in School

Cheryl Craig

In this chapter, I tell the story of another beginning teacher, Tim. I began to work collaboratively with Tim in October 1990, when he was in his first year of teaching. Our shared inquiry continued until 1992.

Tim began teaching in a grade-5 classroom at Kirkpatrick School, a large urban school. Like many beginning teachers, Tim was on a temporary contract. He had completed a Bachelor of Arts degree in Psychology and had worked for two years as a child care worker with problem children. He returned to university and completed his Bachelor of Education degree in 1990. He, like Sonia and Benita, was a student in the alternative program. I came to know Tim through one of our teachers, Jean Clandinin. Both Tim and I had been Jean's students at different times.

During the time of our work together, Tim awakened to the healthy-school story at Kirkpatrick School. In this chapter, I revisit aspects of Tim's told story and make connections between it and the sacred theory-practice story that shaped his first two years of teaching. Two excerpts, one featuring the genesis of the story, the other featuring shifts in Tim's knowledge, are described.

THE HEALTHY SCHOOL, YEAR 1: TIM LIVES AND LEARNS TO TELL A SCHOOL STORY

Tim was not placed in his first teaching position until after the opening days of school. As a teacher arriving late on the scene, Tim lived a school story shaped by others and he was left trying to find his place in it, as he indicated in this excerpt:

> I am just kind of sitting in the background right now. . . . I can tell there are some teachers on staff who agree with administrative poli-

> cies and practices and some people do not. . . . I am just kind of staying in the background this year. . . . There's some strong personalities and very strong people. (Conversation, October 27, 1990)

Tim began to construct a story based on his initial observations and experiences. Tim initially felt "obligated" to engage in extracurricular activities and events (Conversation, December 11, 1991). He observed what other teachers were doing and assumed he also had to do the activities. Tim was shaped by the staff's behavior and came to describe his experience as being "on the treadmill."

> He said he was left with a question: How did he ever survive the first year of teaching? . . . Tim said he was so much a part of it, he could not see it. He mentioned the expression of not seeing the forest for the trees. Tim said that metaphor most aptly described how he felt about the "treadmill." (Field notes, November 8, 1991)

The abundance of school activities both consumed and perplexed Tim. Near the end of his first year of teaching, he questioned another teacher about the purpose of the activities. The teacher responded: "Teachers have to do all these activities for Kirkpatrick school to be a healthy school. Schools where these activities do not occur are dead schools" (Conversation, May 30, 1991).

The school story she shared ascribed the notion of health, usually associated with people, to an institution, the school. The school's health was measured by the activities in which the people engaged. Connections between the school story and a commonly shared story within this particular school system were evident. Kirkpatrick had a long history of involvement in school system projects. Schools involved in projects were viewed as healthy places. At the system level, an association between participation/activity and health was made.

The teacher's answer to Tim's question became the topic of conversations Tim continued to have with himself and with me. This was the beginning of Tim's awakening to a school story he was living.

Tim did not agree with the knowledge the teacher shared with him. His unspoken reply to her interpretation of the healthy-school story was "Better dead schools than dead teachers!" Tim felt teachers had been doing too much. "I think you can do enough and there is a point beyond which it's too much" (Conversation, July 3, 1991). The healthy-school story did not fit with Tim's experience in his first year of teaching. He felt the tension that the constant planning and living of activities created for him and his colleagues. Tim did not like living in a healthy school where his "days wrapped around each other without a spare moment" (Conversation, November 28, 1991). Tim thought activities in the school needed to be reviewed.

After this conversation, Tim began to question his knowledge. Because the teacher was more experienced and had been at the school for a number of years, he felt she was in a better position to know the situation. Tim did not have her breadth of experience, experience that, from his beginning-teacher perspective, seemed to privilege her knowing. Tim discounted his knowledge when her knowledge was mentioned: "I do not know, I mean I am just a new teacher, okay?" (Conversation, May 30, 1991).

But later Tim found support for his views. Some "experienced teachers in our school felt there was too much. So if people like Joyce and Rhonda who will do anything are getting burnt out, we need to step back and take a look at the problem" (Conversation, July 3, 1991). Joyce and Rhonda had taught at Kirkpatrick for over 10 years and had enthusiastically participated in many school activities. They were "unofficial leaders," "cornerstone people," "two of the most 'positive' people on staff" (Conversation, July 3, 1991). Tim understood Joyce's and Rhonda's places in the school context. Their fatigue became part of how he made sense of what his other colleague had said about the healthy school.

Tim also relied on Victor, the school principal, to validate his knowledge. Tim noted Victor's response to school activities:

> *Tim:* At the end of the year . . . on the organizational day Victor said he had a concern about the number of things we have been doing. Not the quality or anything like that, but just the number of things we were doing. . . . (Conversation, July 3, 1991)

Victor's identification of the "problem" fit with Tim's knowing of the situation, validated Tim's knowledge, and lent credibility to his understanding. This gave Tim confidence, and our conversation continued:

> *Cheryl:* . . . all year you always had something to do in addition to teaching.
>
> *Tim:* Always, always . . . I said my perception was that people were very tired and it was because of the overlap of major events and activities.
>
> *Cheryl:* Yes, because you had reporting periods and interviews overlapping with the activities and events.
>
> *Tim:* So we need to see the whole thing. . . as a big picture rather than piece by piece. (Conversation, July 3, 1991)

Tim named the problem as too many activities, overlapping activities, and planning difficulties. One of Tim's colleagues who offered a story about staff change illuminated the problems Tim was coming to know. She mentioned teachers pursuing activities without communicating their intentions to the administration or the rest of the staff. It seemed the "pieces" Tim was mentioning were the activities that individual teachers or groups of teachers were doing that, along with the academic program, "overlapped" one another. "A big picture," as Tim put it, had not been collaboratively agreed on.

Having named the overabundance of activities as a difficulty, Tim was able to see an overabundance of meetings as a manifestation of the problem. In his first year, Tim was involved in grade meetings, division meetings, staff meetings, organizational and professional days, and special-day planning sessions. Tim realized that the meetings did not relate to his teaching. He described his feelings this way:

> I felt most of my time was focused on group goals or school goals or some kind of common task. . . not so much our teaching practices. . . there was not a lot of individual sharing about what was going on in my classroom or in my situation, about how I am thinking about teaching right now. (Conversation, August 3, 1991)

Tim felt he gathered with other teachers to discuss topics of common interest concerning the school's health. Personal teaching experiences seldom were a part of the "agendas." Meetings were not places at which teachers were open to each other's teaching experiences. Viewed through Tim's tree-and-forest metaphor, Tim and his colleagues were engaged in the setting up or living of the next "tree" in a "forest" of activities contributing to the "healthy school." In meetings, Tim felt immersed in trees with no view of the forest. This description resonated with Tim's talk about the staff working with "pieces" rather than the "big picture." Tim turned to questions about how he "survived."

While Tim thought about survival in the healthy-school context, other teachers interpreted his involvement in activities as a sign of health. For example, the teacher who shared Kirkpatrick's story of the healthy school with Tim commented at the end of his first year:

> Tim has learned many things this year, most of which are outside his job description as a teacher. For example, he has been the Master of Ceremonies for the Sports Day Assembly . . . and has been very active in public relations activities such as the School Carnival and the Spring Concert. (Conversation, June 12, 1991)

Tim's development as a teacher was being connected to the healthy school. What Tim did inside his classroom was not visible to others. Conversations about his teaching practices were not shared.

When Tim discussed how his before-school, noon-hour, and after-school time was spent, I asked him whether he needed unstructured time to reflect with his colleagues. Tim responded:

> Oh, yes. Oh, yes. I definitely see a need for it because it all gets back to wellness and reflection. . . . We are doing too much to make time for ourselves and our own professional needs or our own wellness needs. . . . We need time to think about and communicate what we are doing as teachers. . . . Because we are so focused on doing things for other people, we forget about ourselves. (Conversation, August 2, 1991)

Tim introduced the word *wellness*, a school system goal, to our conversations and linked wellness with professional needs. Wellness became his way of thinking about survival in a healthy school. Tim knew if he was not mindful of wellness, his health would be sucked away by the healthy school.

Tim did not openly voice his opinion in his first year of teaching. He privately named reflection as one thing he wished to emphasize in his second year of teaching. Our talk continued:

> *Cheryl:* You spend a lot of time talking about sports day, ice carnival, festival, those kinds of things, things the staff is doing collectively.
>
> *Tim:* Yes, instead of focusing on our own teaching practices. So if there is one thing I would try and push through next year, if the promotion of wellness becomes a committee function, I would try and push or encourage reflection among the staff. It is time for us to just get together to talk about how we are doing. (Conversation, August 2, 1991)

Tim linked reflection with wellness. Even though Tim had kept a journal and engaged in reflective conversations as part of his teacher education experiences, he did not call on this knowledge to support teacher reflection. Instead, Tim connected reflective practices to the healthy school. Tim's sense-making became context-specific, his language particular to his situation in the school and school system. The healthy-school story was subtly shaping his knowledge.

I questioned Tim about the constraints that might hamper his push for reflective practice. At first, he mentioned time, then added: "I guess people need to make a conscious effort to set time aside and say we will do nothing else during this time. . . . I think if people made it a priority . . . it could happen" (Conversation, August 2, 1991). Tim knew that without a "conscious effort" his school staff would be unable to bring reflection and wellness into the healthy-school story. His school staff could change the story only through shared consciousness. He began to try to change the scene. He began to explore other stories to live by.

THE HEALTHY SCHOOL STORY, YEAR 2: THE STAFF ATTEMPTS TO RESTORY THE STORY

On August 29, 1991, and on September 13, 1991, the Kirkpatrick staff held group organizational meetings that would affect the way their story would be lived out that year. On September 13, 1991, Victor formally presented the school mission statement: "to develop a regenerative work environment which will ensure high quality student education and professional wellness." The school system adopted Cahoon's (1991) notion of a "regenerative work environment" and fashioned its mission statement around it. Hence, Victor was not able to create spaces for the staff to contribute to shaping the school's mission statement. Victor's position as a school principal meant he delivered it to the teachers as received knowledge (Belenky et al., 1986), knowledge the leadership team received from the school system, who had received it from a university person. Victor delivered it to the staff and Tim's knowledge was, in turn, shaped by this dissemination of directives filtered through the conduit onto his professional knowledge landscape.

Victor said the staff would be working on a "school action plan." He spoke of the staff "biting off more than could be chewed" and people "pushing themselves to the end of June." He emphasized that the staff was doing too much. Nearing retirement with little to lose in his position in the conduit, Victor invited the staff to restory what Tim had come to know as the healthy-school story. Victor suggested the staff work together "and learn to be realistic and . . . let some things go. . . . We have to think about what we can reasonably accomplish and what we can cooperatively accomplish" (Field notes, September 13, 1991). Victor's description of the problem resonated with Tim's knowledge from his first year of teaching. It also resonated with Tim's desire to focus on reflection and wellness.

The staff began by discussing past, present, and proposed activities. They decided to keep Sports Day, cut down on the number of assemblies, and eliminate the Christmas Concert.

Sports Day, for example, was unquestionably accepted as an important school activity. Some staff members commented on the frantic preparations for Sports Day the previous year. For Tim, however, the previous Sports Day had been a time when, with some staff members tired and others preoccupied, he had an opportunity to shape an activity. Tim felt he "emerged into a leadership role" as he worked with Jonas, the vice-principal, on Sports Day preparations (Conversation, August 3, 1991).

The staff's discussions about Sports Day, assemblies, and the Christmas Concert foreshadowed their discussion of extracurricular events. As individual items were held open for inspection, multiple opinions were offered and time for decision making became increasingly limited.

Some staff members assumed that clubs and sports activities had the same status as Sports Day and would continue. Jonas and Tim made this assumption and wanted to plan for these activities. Their proposed changes fine-tuned the activities of a healthy school. Other staff members, however, had accepted Victor's invitation to seriously review extracurricular practices. These teachers began to explore alternate ways to live in the school. Bonnie, for example, requested that the staff shift their focus from the activities to the students, from the healthy school as an institution to the people in it. Shifting the focus from burnt-out teachers, she passionately spoke of "burnt-out kids . . . inundated by activities."

Dolores then asked a critical question: "How many things are we going to do?" Jonas mentioned the teachers' unvoiced fear of criticism from the community: "We will hear from the parents." Some teachers then downplayed the tasks of organizing house leagues. But Dolores was undeterred and again reminded the staff that activities took lots of planning and lots of time. Jonas returned to his knowledge of the healthy school and refocused their attention on the organization of the activities. Bonnie interjected, "Something has to go." Bonnie and I later talked and I recorded her thoughts on the issue.

> Bonnie said extracurricular practices take teachers away from their teaching practices. She said she would like to have time to talk with other teachers. (Field notes, September 24, 1991)

Bonnie hoped I did not view her as selfish. She spoke in a way that reminded me of a familiar story of feeling guilty about not doing enough.

Tim and Bonnie appeared to have much in common in what they said about the activities in the school. But Tim's story began to be altered in planning for the extracurricular activities and the story continued in unexpected ways.

Shauna, a resource teacher new to the school, entered the conversation and supported Bonnie's position. Tim then tried to downplay the time commitment of clubs. Shauna repeated that the staff had to limit its activities. She said she knew about the stress associated with the activities of the healthy school. She reminded everyone that she had toured the school the previous year when they were worn out from overinvolvement. Victor had also shared with her the problems of teacher stress and absenteeism.

Fran, also new to the staff and unaware of the school's history, disagreed with Shauna. Fran disapproved of the staff's making decisions for individuals. Bonnie then disagreed with Fran, explaining that activities did not happen "in isolation like teaching." Bonnie hinted that school decisions should not be made by individuals. She reminded her colleagues that teaching was their primary responsibility. Again, Bonnie was suggesting an alternative way to live in a healthy school.

Teachers who had previously not voiced their opinions entered the conversation. They indicated that they felt guilty when they did not meet the demands placed on them. As more female teachers voiced their opinions, Bonnie reminded the staff that they needed to change how they were living. Bonnie's suggestions did not fit with Jonas' knowledge of the healthy-school story. Jonas' comments called forth a feeling of guilt from many of the teachers. He stated that teachers were showing preference for their wellness at the expense of the wellness of the students. The staff, however, voted to have club activities one year and extracurricular events the next.

In this discussion, I anticipated that Tim would situate himself with teachers whose knowledge seemed compatible with the sense-making he had shared with me in the summer. I was surprised when Tim expressed displeasure with this decision of the staff. As I reflected on it, there were two ways I could make sense of Tim's not agreeing with the decision. One way was looking at the staff decision as "an overreaction to the treadmill." Overreaction suggests overcorrection and was not consistent with Tim's desire for balance. The staff had made a decision that appeared to favor teachers over students and Tim wanted the issue taken back to the staff for further deliberation. The second way I could make sense of Tim's not agreeing with the decision had to do with a story Jonas was telling, a story Tim caught a glimpse of when he was involved in Sports Day activities.

Let me explore the first way of making sense of Tim's decision to take the decision back to the staff for further deliberation. Tim next spoke with two prominent members of his school staff: Jonas and Marj. Jonas was a friend and had publicly expressed his discontent with how the staff was attempting to restory the healthy-school story. Jonas agreed with Tim's concern and confirmed Tim's knowledge of the situation. Tim also took his concern to Marj, whom Tim considered "a wise owl" (Interview 14, May 25, 1991), a teacher with 18 years of teaching experience in the school, a teacher to whom the staff listened. Marj's response to Tim was that individuals should make decisions for themselves. Like Jonas, Marj validated Tim's knowledge.

After consulting Jonas and Marj, Tim appealed to the staff to consider "the school and the students and how to best balance those needs with our personal well-being." Tim asked his colleagues to remember there were athletic and nonathletic students in the school and sports events one year and club activities the next year would not meet the needs of the whole student population. When the staff reconsidered the decision, they agreed with Tim by a 14–10 margin. In this sense, Tim influenced the staff decision.

Viewed from a different perspective, however, Tim was expressing his knowledge of how the healthy-school story had shaped his practices. Rather than using imposed time constraints to build his argument for reviewing the staff's decision, Tim reminded his colleagues of the students and the expectation that teachers would provide activities for them. Unwittingly, Tim returned the staff to the healthy-school story. In the process, Tim's colleagues began to feel guilty about reducing the activities in the school and about thinking about their own well-being first. As Marj explained:

> The reassessment made the guilt trip set in with the staff and soon people were saying: "Well, if so and so is going to do this, then I should be doing something too. . . ." She said teachers' egos were involved. (Conversation, September 24, 1991)

Marj's explanation reminded me of the "one upmanship" of which Bonnie had spoken earlier and of Dolores' reference in another conversation to "the ego enhancement of teachers." Marj sensed the staff was heading toward "a repetition of the same kinds of activities as last year" (Conversation, September 24, 1991).

Tim's appeal to the staff also confused Victor. It was contrary to the earlier conversations he had had with Tim about activities. Victor wondered why Tim had become so focused on activities and committee work (Field notes, October 22, 1991). It seems that Victor was so close to the situation he could not see how powerfully the healthy-school story had shaped Tim's knowledge.

Tim felt his appeal to the staff ended in "a nice compromise" (Conversation, September 24, 1991). At the same time Tim was thinking this thought, other teachers were voicing their opinions in the staff room: "I heard comments, some rumblings about returning to the same old activities, and the belief that there were too many activities going on in the school" (Conversation, September 24, 1991).

It appeared that Tim was unaware of the sense other teachers were making of the healthy-school story. He did not have spaces to enter into conversations with them nor they with him or each other. Tim continued to filter his knowledge through the healthy-school story. Through that lens, teachers not participating in activities were not fulfilling their responsibilities to the students and the school. Tim did not see particular teachers' intentionally removing themselves from healthy-school activities to reclaim conversations about educational practice. He did not recognize the alternative school story he had entertained during the summer months. Tim saw himself involved in "more than an average" number of activities. He assessed Jonas' situation in the same way. Tim took on more activities to reduce the load Jonas was carrying, and contributed more to school activities in his second year of teaching than in his first (Field notes, May 25, 1992). Tim ended up working extremely hard to keep the healthy-school story alive.

Before continuing this line of thinking, I wish to return for a time to consider another story, the one Jonas was defending, the one Tim was beginning to know. Tim defined his place in the school by his positions and his activities. Toward the end of his first year, he was heavily involved in planning Sports Day with Jonas. Tim associated Jonas' participation in extracurricular activities with his administrative role. Working with Jonas on Sports Day was the beginning of what Tim termed his "growth into leadership" and Tim wished to "continue the momentum." The leadership experience subtly shaped Tim's knowledge. As leadership became part of Tim's knowing, his knowledge of the healthy-school story shifted. He became more accommodating of the story:

> This theme has . . . to do with all those things we feel will create a "healthy" school. Thinking back to the comment I was told about "dead schools," my response then would have been "Better dead schools than dead teachers!" Now, I am changing my perspective slightly. I think back to the beginning of this year when certain extracurricular activities were left out because the staff was overreacting to the "treadmill." It was I who advocated for nonathletic students and brought about a reassessment of what we really wanted to do. This was another very significant occurrence which contributed to my growth. (Tim's response to stories.)

Tim recognized the shift in his "perspective" and his restorying of the healthy-school story. He also viewed his contribution to the staff reassessment of school activities as part of his "growth." Previously when Tim used the word *growth,* he had connected it with leadership: "growth into leadership" (Conversation, August 3, 1991). Other responses Tim made also pointed to shifts in the story he was beginning to tell.

> I have indeed found a "place" on staff in several areas this year: the New Teacher Group, the Teachers' Association representative, Committee work on two committees: Professional Development and Extra-Curricular, and the Computer Coordinator for the school. I know this is a lot when you consider what the average teacher . . . does, or is willing to do. I am full of enthusiasm and I want to be on the "leading edge" in our school. (Tim's response to stories.)

Tim continued to use leadership vocabulary to express his knowledge. To be on the "leading edge," Tim organized committees and activities for "the healthy school." These activities and positions put Tim on the "inside track" in the school (Conversation, May 25, 1992). Tim had come to know the "getting ahead" and "leadership" stories embedded in the healthy-school story. He restoried his knowledge of the healthy school as other stories of personal possibility became apparent to him.

About the same time that Tim was highly involved in Sports Day planning, he wrote a reflective piece titled "Children's Stories." Tim shared his narrative with Helga, another young teacher in the school, and hoped she might keep a journal with him or serve on a committee with him to address "the isolation we face as teachers" (July 9, 1991). Unfortunately, Tim's hopes to keep a journal with Helga did not materialize due to a lack of time. The second thing Tim did with his reflective piece was to put it in the staff room to share with other teachers. Dolores noticed it but no one read it. What Tim was attempting to do was to share his knowledge as a reflective practitioner in a way that had been cultivated in the professional knowledge landscape of the alternative program. But when Tim attempted to share his stories with his new school staff, they did not respond in the manner he anticipated. Tim felt his knowledge was devalued as his carefully crafted stories became part of a "pile" on the staff-room table that "does not get read" (Conversation, July 9, 1991). This incident occurred about the same time that Tim was introduced to the getting ahead and leadership stories as he worked on Sports Day preparations. Following these two experiences, Tim restoried his knowledge of the healthy-school story. The "reflection and wellness" landscape for which he voiced a preference seemed impossible to cultivate. Tim embraced the healthy-school story as his own.

CONNECTING TIM'S HEALTHY-SCHOOL STORY TO THE SACRED STORY IN SCHOOLS

As Tim made his transition from university to school, he moved between two different places on the professional knowledge landscape. In one place, the alternative program, reflection was valued; in the other place, Kirkpatrick School, action was valued. Tim's acknowledgment of these different places on the landscape is important in understanding his narrative of experience. Even when Tim realized the need for reflection in the school context, he did not call forth his university experiences to support his knowing. Tim tacitly knew about the competing epistemologies (Schon, 1992) that framed the views of knowledge in each institution. He couched his desire for reflection in the "wellness" language of the school system. He knew his suggestion had to be grounded in the school system's way of knowing. Otherwise, it would be rejected because it was out of place.

As a beginning teacher, Tim was very vulnerable. He learned to be silent and to mirror what experienced teachers were doing. In this way he lived a cover story. As his first year of teaching ended and his second began, he began to know that regular teachers and classroom practice were not often acknowledged or valued in the transmission of knowledge and in the moral imperatives delivered through the conduit.

Tim found that the focus was often on the functions of the staff within the school and not on teachers with their students in classrooms. Tim began to know that his worth as a teacher was attached to the activities he contributed to the school rather than to his teaching. He found himself involved in an increasing number of activities outside his classroom to demonstrate his worth to the school. Tim knew that this involvement would help him build his professional profile (the practical equivalent of a curriculum vitae), which would be useful to him when he applied for future leadership positions in the school system.

When Tim wrote his teacher narrative, a practice he learned in the alternative program, he identified the tension he felt between the alternative program and the school, the two places where he had been cultivated. By connecting reflection, an aspect of the alternative-program context, and wellness, an aspect of the school system context, Tim was suggesting a competing story of the theory-practice relationship. He was trying to outline the plot for a new story to live by in his school. However, as events progressed, Tim learned that this new imagined story was not a part of the healthy-school story. Rewards were directly attached to the healthy school and Tim chose to return to it.

When the school mission statement was presented to the staff, it came to the teachers as a piece of received knowledge, a kind of "rhetoric of conclusions" stripped of the inquiry that created it (Schwab, 1962). The knowledge was dictated to practice as a kind of "the research says . . ." document. The mission statement was constructed and wound its way through the school system, ending with teachers who were expected to absorb the dictates into their practices. Bonnie noted that teachers felt both pressure and obligation to make these change efforts a part of their knowledge because they were required to defend them to the public.

In the staff discussions, we see the genesis of a story that competes with the healthy-school story. Bonnie and some other staff members suggest a competing story of how to live in the school, a story similar to Tim's first-year telling. Bonnie warned me that this competing story could be interpreted as teacher selfishness, an interpretation that would make the story a conflicting one. As Bonnie predicted, Jonas voiced this view when he defended the healthy-school story in staff discussions. Tim also alluded to selfishness in his final defense of the healthy-school story. In addition, Tim argued that the reduction and restructuring of student activities resulted in a slate of activities designed for exclusive groups of students—the athletic group one year, the nonathletic group the following year. Some staff members saw selfishness and exclusivity as outside the range of acceptable stories of educational practice and changed their votes. The negative connotations served to squelch the competing story and, without a viable alternative, the staff returned to the healthy-school story, which framed the moral horizons of Kirkpatrick School's professional knowledge landscape.

Toward the end of his second year of teaching, Tim recognized the reward system within his school and within the school district. He learned about the "inside track" as he undertook extracurricular activities. By involving himself in activities and by taking on positions, Tim knew he would be valued in the school district. Tim's male colleagues had shared these stories with him. Tim also knew this story from watching female teachers like Joyce, who were highly involved in school and school system activities and who were promoted to leadership positions. Tim opted into the healthy-school story, in part, because it offered him promising possibilities for the future.

CONCLUSION

In Tim's story there are manifestations of the sacred theory-practice story that are rarely made visible. They powerfully shape the moral horizons he came to know in his professional knowledge landscape. Tim's healthy-school story shows how he imagines the possibility for a competing story but abandons it when he sees that rewards and recognition are his if he subscribes to a particular version of the healthy school. He withdraws from telling a competing version of the healthy-school story when he realizes how easily the story can become a conflicting one, a story that could marginalize him on the out-of-classroom place in his professional knowledge landscape.

CHAPTER 9

Beginning Teaching: Stories of Position, and Positioning, on the Landscape

D. Jean Clandinin and F. Michael Connelly

The previous two chapters portray two dramatically different beginning teacher stories. Benita's story, lived out in many different classrooms as a substitute teacher (Chapter 7), is a story of learning how to be a good classroom teacher. Tim's story, lived out on one school's landscape (Chapter 8), is a story of learning how to find a place among school colleagues. Though we do not discuss it here, Tim also has a story of learning to be a good classroom teacher (Craig, 1992). The stories told in our chapters are dramatically different in the language used, in the things talked about and thought about, and in the places on the landscape where the action took place. It is a difference of Benita's image of a good teacher and Tim's metaphor of the healthy school; it is a difference of Benita's concern for children and what she learned about being a good teacher from them and Tim's concern for situating himself relative to the school mission statement; it is a difference of the in-classroom place on the professional knowledge landscape for Benita and the out-of-classroom place on the professional knowledge landscape for Tim.

Initially, looking at this from a distance, we registered surprise. Benita and Tim had both been part of a strong competing story of an alternative program of teacher education. We might have assumed that this participation in the alternative program would contribute to a shared narrative unity of teaching that would carry over into their professional lives. Yet there is very little similarity between their stories of the first years of teaching. The stories of their development as teachers diverged from a common reference point in the alternative program through their first years of teaching. The obvious difference between the two, the one having a substitute teaching position and the other having a full-time position, gives a superficial explanation of this divergence. But it is a close-up examination of the development of their professional knowledge during the first years of teaching that makes it possible to understand this divergence in terms of the relationship of personal practical and professional knowledge. In the remainder of the chapter, we explore this understanding.

CONTEXTUALIZING THE PERSONAL PRACTICAL WITH THE PROFESSIONAL

To develop this understanding, we need to return to the question of Chapter 1, that is, the question of how teachers' personal practical knowledge interacts with the professional knowledge landscape. We said that our general purpose was to explore how the context of teaching influenced teachers' personal practical knowledge of teaching. In Benita's and Tim's cases the contexts differ. Benita's knowledge is contextualized in a series of different classrooms. Tim's knowledge is contextualized in a single classroom and its out-of-classroom place on the landscape. In broad outlines, our explanation hinges on our sense that participation in the same alternative program would have created strong common elements in Benita's and Tim's personal practical knowledge. Yet their knowledge developed in strikingly different ways. We want to argue that this happened because of how Benita and Tim were positioned, and positioned themselves, on the professional knowledge landscape.

They participated in the same alternative teacher education program. They spent time together with the same group of university teachers, cooperating teachers, and student teachers. They taught in different student teaching settings but shared their stories during group sessions. We would expect that these conditions would conspire to create a shared, more or less common, story of teaching for Benita and Tim. Furthermore, that story would undoubtedly have been strengthened by the fact that both Benita and Tim are participants in the studies reported in this book. The influence of these experiences in shaping their personal practical knowledge is evident in both Chapter 5 and Chapter 7 accounts of Benita, where she writes journals and stories for her portfolio, and in the Chapter 8 account of Tim, where he writes the reflective pieces that he leaves in the staff room in an attempt to stimulate conversations among teachers. Both of these activities are consistent with what might be expected of a teacher graduate of the alternative program.

The first indication of divergence in Benita and Tim's teacher stories shows up in the first year of teaching, where differences in their positions on the professional knowledge landscape are evident and begin to assert their influences. Benita begins her teaching as a substitute teacher. This positions her on many in-classroom places on the professional knowledge landscape. Her focus is on contextualizing her personal practical knowledge in different classrooms. What we see in Benita's story is what we expect from new teachers, that is, to be primarily concerned with her classroom teaching. Broadly speaking, a new teacher's concerns tend to be more with matters dealing with the in-classroom place on the professional knowledge landscape than with the out-of-classroom place. In part, this focus on the in-classroom place is the only focus Benita can have because she is a substitute teacher. She fits in no one classroom and cannot get involved with schoolwide activities. She has no place on any out-of-classroom professional knowledge landscape.

Tim, in his first year, is positioned very differently on the professional knowledge landscape. He is a teacher with a particular in-classroom place on the landscape. He is also a teacher in a school that has a particular out-of-classroom landscape. In his first year, Tim is also primarily concerned with contextualizing his personal practical knowledge in the classroom (Craig, 1992). However, he also begins to contextualize his personal practical knowledge wth his out-of-classroom work with the school Sports Day and other school activities. At the end of the first year, he is concerned with the toll that the work on the out-of-classroom place on the landscape is taking. He says, "There is a point beyond which it is too much." His response to the sense of being overloaded is, however, a turning point in the direction of his professional development. At the beginning of his second year of teaching, these out-of-classroom activities begin to take hold of his concerns and dominate his interests. As we follow this, we see Tim first starting to experience the dilemma of crossing the boundary.

FINDING A POSITION ON THE LANDSCAPE

In Chapter 1, we described epistemological differences between the in-classroom and the out-of-classroom places on the professional knowledge landscape. Teachers cross the boundary between a safe place for living the secret stories of teaching to a place of moral persuasion and abstract knowledge. This creates a moral and an epistemological dilemma. Tim became aware of this dilemma at the end of his first year of teaching, just prior to beginning his second year. He framed the dilemma by saying that he felt that too much of his time was "focused on group goals or school goals" and not enough on "what was going on in my classroom." Chapter 8 presents, in part, an account of how Tim learned to manage this dilemma. He began by questioning his out-of-classroom work load but shifted direction and became increasingly caught up by the moral persuasiveness of the school story, eventually persuading other teachers to maintain that story. In the following, we work through this transition.

What is the school story? A person walking into Kirkpatrick School would not easily come to know the healthy-school story. It was not named as such, nor was it discussed in the staff room or in meetings, though people did talk about the school's health. But Craig, as researcher, noticed it when Tim began to pay serious attention to what was going on in the out-of-classroom place on the professional knowledge landscape and to how he was torn between classroom teaching and what was demanded by the school story. In conversation with other teachers, Tim tried to make sense of the purposes of the many out-of-classroom activities. The story was first named when, in response to Tim's questioning, a teacher said, "Teachers have to do all these activities for Kirkpatrick School to be a healthy school." The story clearly carried moral overtones about teacher identity in Kirkpatrick School. Being a character in the healthy-school story was the proper way of living on the professional knowledge landscape of Kirkpatrick School.

Tim, confronted with the dilemma this created for him, began to question the healthy-school story. He felt he did not have the energy to continue to teach and to remain a character in the story. At one point he said, "My perception was that people were very tired and it was because of the overlap of major events and activities." Tim raised his concerns in the school planning deliberations. There were a variety of reactions as people recognized and debated the school story. It became apparent that, for some teachers, the healthy-school story was only a cover story. For example, one teacher, Bonnie, said, "Extracurricular practices take teachers away from their teaching practices." Another teacher, Marj, clearly believing in Bonnie's view, shows the sense in which teachers such as herself and Bonnie lived a cover story at Kirkpatrick when she said, "Well, if so and so is going to do this, then I should be doing something too." For others, it was not a cover story. For them, the healthy-school story had become a story of who they were as teachers, and this, as we show below, is Tim's eventual story. As Tim's questioning proceeded, it became apparent that some teachers had learned to tell the healthy-school story outside their classrooms as a cover story. Others had adopted the story as their own and lived the healthy-school story as part of their personal practical and professional knowledge.

Some teachers pointed out that the idea of a healthy school was given to them by the school jurisdiction. It came to them via the conduit. Though we have no record of a specific board policy on this, some teachers felt, as one teacher said, that "schools where these activities do not occur are dead schools," implying a system story. This story is also traceable to the school's mission statement, shaped by the central office, which refers to developing "a regenerative work environment which will ensure higher quality student education and professional wellness." A careful reader of Chapter 8 will notice that the staff, supported by the principal, Victor, temporarily overturned the healthy-school story. The quick return to it is undoubtedly influenced by their recognition that the story is a story given by the conduit. By a vote of 14 to 10, the teachers reaffirmed the healthy-school story. But the vote does not tell us how people positioned themselves on the landscape. To know that we need to know each individual teacher's story.

A school visitor would not be able to tell the difference between teachers who lived the school story as a cover story and those who lived it as part of their identity. Everyone, whether they believed they had to do it for success and promotion or for survival, lived the same story. We see how Tim, after identifying the story and deliberately trying to interrupt it in conversation with others, eventually learns to make the story his own. He said, "Now I'm changing my perspective slightly . . . I have indeed found a 'place' on staff"—and here he named a list of activities on the out-of-classroom place on the landscape. For Tim, it is not a cover story. It became part of his identity, the proper way to be a teacher.

We now wish to speculate on the role of Cheryl Craig as researcher in this story. Our picture is that there was a school story buried in the out-of-classroom place on the professional knowledge landscape. This story played a significant moral role in the professional activities of teachers. The story was named in a conversation between Tim and a teacher. In the ordinary course of events, it is probable that this naming of the story would have passed more or less unnoticed. Cheryl made an issue out of it. Her discussions with Tim on this point undoubtedly shaped Tim's sense of what it was that was troubling him and about which he wanted to engage other teachers in conversation. We cannot know how this story would have evolved without Cheryl's presence, but her presence clearly influenced Tim, the development of the story in the school as Tim pursued his questioning, and our understanding of the nature of professional knowledge landscape stories.

SEARCHING FOR A POSITION ON THE LANDSCAPE

Whereas Tim was positioned, and positioned himself, on the landscape in such a way as to create a sense of identity, Benita was positioned, and positioned herself, in such a way that she lived a series of cover stories. Earlier in this chapter, we sketched Benita's story of working as a substitute teacher. We noted that her focus was on contextualizing her personal practical knowledge in many different in-classroom places. It is important to note that these classrooms were not her own. She was positioned in them as a visitor. What she experienced as a substitute teacher was her attempt to contextualize her personal practical knowledge within secret classroom stories lived by other teachers.

For Benita, the classroom was not a secret place. We did, of course, argue in Chapter 1 that classrooms were secret places for living secret stories. Yet, for Benita, a substitute teacher, this was not the case. She felt quite strongly that she had to teach in a certain way. She knew that the stories that would be told of her by children, by teachers with whom she was team-teaching, and by the homeroom teacher to whom students would report would make quite visible her stories of teaching. She could not hope to act in a way in the classroom that ran counter to what she imagined to be the accepted and required ways. This created a special kind of dilemma for Benita because, as she worked hard to develop and ground her image of herself as a teacher, she had to act in ways that fit a variety of other teachers' stories. In a sense, she lived multiple cover stories. In contrast, when Tim might also have been expected to still be grounding his image of himself in his classroom, he was, instead, crossing the boundary and focusing on his position on the out-of-classroom place on the landscape. Benita had no ongoing position on the landscape of any one school, either in or out of the classroom.

SUMMARY

Tim was positioned on both places on the landscape in a single school. Benita was positioned only on the in-classroom place and in a series of schools. This difference in how they were positioned influenced their active positioning of themselves as time passed and had dramatic consequences for their sense of identity as teachers. Tim experienced a dilemma between the demands of the classroom and the demands outside it. These out-of-classroom demands of the professional knowledge landscape were encased in a healthy-school story that defined the moral horizons for creating a sense of teacher identity in his school. After a period of personal inquiry into the dilemma, Tim chose to position himself in a certain way on the landscape, thereby resolving the dilemma. Because Tim made the school story his own, he became confirmed in his identity as a teacher. Benita experienced a dilemma between the classroom teacher she wanted to be and the classroom teacher she believed she had to be in order to be successful in her changing classroom assignments. She positioned herself by choosing to adapt her teaching to what she thought was expected of her in the series of classrooms. This creation of a series of cover stories made it possible for her to succeed as a substitute teacher but left her with a sense of unease about her identity as a teacher. As she ended the year she said, "I lose faith in myself."

PART IV

PROFESSIONAL KNOWLEDGE LANDSCAPES OF TEACHING

CHAPTER 10

Two Competing Stories of Professional Development

Pat Hogan

I was home from school with a cold when Stacey, my team partner, called following a staff meeting at the school. "You won't believe what happened! They called our group a clique and said there was no place for such exclusivity at our school." I could hear the hurt and bewilderment in Stacey's voice. I, too, was confused and upset by the story she told about what had transpired at the meeting. "They've decided that the three professional-development groups will be disbanded and three new groups will be formed. People will be randomly assigned to their new groups." Stacey and I talked for some time on the telephone, trying to figure out what was going on among members of our staff. We wondered what we had done wrong and how we had managed to offend people outside our group.

The idea to set up three small professional-development groups in our school came from our principal during her first year in the school, the year prior to my arrival on staff. She had seen a presentation on differentiated professional development and was interested in ways to involve the diversity of perspectives she saw within the members of the staff. The staff responded favorably to the idea and a few staff members visited another school, which had tried differentiated professional development. Later, the entire staff worked through a process of examining beliefs and identifying three topics or areas of interest for professional development. Individual members of the staff signed up for one of the three groups. At the beginning of the following year, the groups met to decide on how they might proceed to explore their topic.

The group that Stacey and I chose, "Teacher as Researcher," decided to write reflective journals about our teaching and our classrooms. We would find someone in the group with whom we could share our journals and receive some response. Then we would get together about once a month to talk about the things we were trying to figure out in our practice.

The early meetings in our group were tentative affairs. We did not yet know who in the group we could trust or what kind of talk would be seen as politically correct. I felt especially tentative about how I might be seen by other members of the group. I sensed that, as a newcomer to the school and as a recent university teacher and a former consultant to the system, I might be seen as someone with an administrative perspective. I was eager to dispel such a myth and to establish myself as a teacher among teachers. I began to speak frankly about some of the things that I was noticing and that were bothering me about the ways things were done at our school. My early comments were met with some suspicion and concern that our meetings might turn into "bitch sessions," but gradually, as we continued meeting (and broke down some of the inhibitions over wine), we began to risk saying some of the things we cared deeply about in our teaching and in our school. We began to trust each other and to engage in what I call "real talk."

After our first year together, we asked that our group remain intact. I think we had a sense we were just beginning something that needed more time to develop. Our request was supported by the principal and we felt encouraged by comments from other staff members who wanted to know more about what we were doing and about how we functioned together as a group. At the time we did not really have words to describe how we worked together but we explained as best we could and the other two groups began to talk about writing reflective journals, as we were doing.

In our second year together, I had a sense of our voices strengthening. We received courage from one another and began to raise some of our concerns in staff meetings and with the school administrators. We looked to each other for support at meetings and referred to the discussions we had with each other within the group. At one meeting, a staff member from another group commented that she felt "left out" of the kind of talk we were experiencing. I did not know quite what to make of this comment. I tried to be reassuring and made some extra efforts to be friendly but I do not really think I heard what she was saying.

Because I had not heard any threat to our group in those words, Stacey's telephone call came as a great surprise to me. I could not understand the accusations about exclusivity and cliques. I was frustrated and hurt. Because I was still home from school with a cold, I reacted with an angry letter to the administration. I wrote about my thoughts after reading *Meeting at the Crossroads* (Mikel Brown & Gilligan, 1992) and said:

> I cannot help but relate these thoughts to the issue of our P.D. groups. For me, participation in the same group over two years has brought us to a place where we are able to freely voice our thoughts and feelings, speak openly and honestly. Within the group this has meant the formation of many real relationships. It occurs to me that this feeling within the group might be the "exclusivity" that those outside the group are naming and resenting. If this is the case I feel sad and discouraged. The proposed solution is equally discouraging. I could accept a decision on the part of the staff to move to a new type of P.D. activity but I cannot understand reorganizing the groups. I don't know how we can claim to be collaborative and to honor teacher voice at our school and then turn around and break up a group that is functioning in these ways. To me, it's an act of silencing.
>
> I also recognize that mine is not the only voice in this decision. If everyone on staff wants this reorganization of P.D. groups then I expect that we will reorganize. If this is the case, I'd like to be in a group that is interested in exploring issues of voice. I'd like to look at children's, parents' and teachers' voices—at how we make spaces for the voices and at how they are silenced.

I received a telephone call from the principal in response to my letter. She had not been at the staff meeting either and she invited me to talk with her about the situation when I returned to school. Later, in her office, we spoke about the changes that were occurring on our staff and about the move to teaming that was demanding so much energy from staff members. At the next staff meeting, the principal raised the issue of how a decision had been made to reorganize professional-development groups. Some members of the staff complained that a decision had already been reached. I tried to verbalize some of the concerns I had raised in my letter but I suspect only my anger was conveyed. The meeting was spent discussing the concept with each person being asked, in turn, to voice an opinion. All were invited to respond in writing to the principal about how they would like to see professional-development time spent. In the end, the decision to randomly assign people to new groups was abandoned, along with the whole notion of small-group professional development. Instead there would be more time for team planning among class groups.

AN ATTEMPT AT RETELLING

As I look back on the story lived and told some months ago, I remember the sense of hopelessness and despair that surrounded me and permeated my relationships with other teachers in the school. In the days following Stacey's phone call, I talked with her about the situation but we could think of nothing that gave us any sense of being able to change the attitudes or actions that were angering and hurting us. Other members of our group were concerned, but not nearly as upset as we were. A couple of them responded to the accusations with an inclination to change groups in order to avoid any hard feelings. We felt isolated from the rest of the staff and bewildered by how differently they seemed to view the events and our reactions to those events. As Stacey and I tried to figure things out, we imagined other members of the staff experiencing feelings of jealousy and competition and we tried to imagine what we had done to cause those feelings. We even spoke of trying to transfer out of the school.

I could not begin to see any reason or hope until I'd had several conversations with Jean, Annie, and Cheryl. In those conversations, my thoughts were turned to the professional dynamics of my school. This helped me shift what was happening from a personal attack to how a group of teachers working in a common professional setting could collectively create points of conflict. I began to talk about the people, the events, and my reactions in ways that began to make some sense to me. In many ways, this new language expanded my horizons. It allowed me to see what had transpired in a different light, a light that illuminated a larger picture. I began to realize that the story I had originally told was missing some essential parts, and now I find I need to add to the original text in order to convey my new understanding. I am wondering now if understanding means being able to use a richer language to tell a more complete story. Perhaps if I'd had some of this language to talk with my group and with other members of the staff about the story we were trying to live, we might have avoided some of the difficulties. I now need to go back and understand the story as one set within a professional knowledge landscape.

The idea that schools are organized around an epistemology came to me from Don Schön (1992). That idea helped me to see our school in a particular light. The view of knowledge as received, expert, and hierarchical is widely accepted in our school, in other schools within our board, and in the society in which we live. Because it is seldom called into question, it becomes a sacred story within the professional knowledge landscape.

The sacred story is lived and told in professional-development activities over and over again. Often a school will invite a speaker from outside to inform the staff on a particular program or topic. At other times a person with expertise will be invited to conduct a workshop on a new program or methodology. Sometimes a paper written by an academic will serve to initiate a discussion among staff members. This, I suspect, was the accepted way to conduct professional development at our school before the three professional-development groups were formed. It is a strong story and it is understandable that it continued to be lived out by two of the three professional-development groups that were formed at our school. I vaguely remember the other two groups inviting people to share their expertise or to conduct workshops on a topic. I also remember teachers from the other groups visiting sites where particular programs were in place and returning to our school to attempt to implement those programs in our setting. I recognize this story well because, for many years, it was my story. I had worked as a consultant and played the role of outside expert in many settings. I had directed teachers to visit classrooms and schools where innovative programs were in place. I had lived the sacred story and eventually come to question the idea that knowledge resides outside of practice, outside of classroom teachers. I also could see how this idea is so dominant in our system that it becomes the story that is lived out even when the format for professional development changes.

I believe that our group tried to live a story that was in competition with the sacred story. Instead of looking for knowledge from outside ourselves, we were attempting to recognize and value the knowledge held by teachers within the group. This competing story was not one we could adequately describe in words. We tried to be together in new ways and eventually began to engage in "real talk." While Stacey and I viewed the talk as the most important aspect of our work, there were other members of our group who felt a little guilty about how we spent our time. Perhaps they were responding to the questions and comments I had previously failed to understand. Perhaps they saw that our talk was being noticed and the different story we were living was being recognized. The other teachers in our group visited the professional library when one of the other groups was doing research. These teachers in our group sought out articles to bring to our meetings. Yet we rarely engaged in sustained conversation with the research. Our talk returned to stories of practice. I now see how their library visits could be seen as evidence that they were caught between the dominant story and the competing one. What we were attempting to do interrupted the dominant story and the reaction, which once baffled me, now makes more sense. I began to see the response to our attempt to live a new story of professional development as one that comes out of a moral horizon different from my own. I believed that the best professional development comes out of a horizon that values our own knowledge for teacher growth.

The incident in our school over professional-development groups seems now like a bit of a lesson to me in how moral horizons are called on and used to prevent any real changes from occurring in the contexts in which we work. When we set up professional-development groups and tried to live a different story in our particular group, we were competing with the story of how professional development should be done in schools. The competing story was tolerated for a time but it eventually turned into a conflicting story and moral justifications were used to have everyone return to the dominant story. The accusations of exclusivity were moral accusations.

In coming to this understanding, I realize there are important details that I omitted from my original story. The year prior to my arrival at the school was the first year for a new principal as well as the year in which preliminary work was undertaken for changing professional development to small-group work. It is difficult for me to assess how those two events are related but I am convinced that they are connected. At the start of this chapter, I noted that the principal favored differentiated professional development, had some of our staff visit an exemplary school, and subsequently held staff meetings to explore possibilities for our school. The three professional-development groups were the result of this process. I believe that the new principal perceived that differentiated professional development would meet the needs and challenges of the school and this, in turn, was central to her story of what it means to be a principal. In her attempts to develop a shared vision with the staff, she saw the proposed change in professional-development format as an opportunity, as she wrote, "to meet the diverse needs of those on staff" and to ensure there was "something for everyone."

From the beginning, we seemed to have our principal's support for how we were conducting our group. She did ask questions from time to time about whether we were "making good use of our time." We were careful to take the time to reassure and inform her as to the value of our talk together. This negotiation, I believe, was crucial to our group's being given support to remain intact for a second year. Yet we had done little to negotiate with the rest of the staff. We failed to read the questions and comments from others as an indication that ours was a competing story. When a new assistant principal arrived at the school during that second year, we also neglected to conduct negotiations with her. As I look back now I can see how that failure on our part was instrumental in the final outcome of abandoning small-group professional development.

When we failed to negotiate with the staff and especially with the new assistant principal about what we were trying to accomplish in our group, we neglected to take some of the steps I have come to believe are necessary to ensure survival of a competing story. The assistant principal chaired the staff meeting at which accusations were made about the exclusivity of our group. I was not there and neither was the principal. The competing story in our small group might have been protected if the principal had chaired the meeting. She seemed to understand and appreciate what we were trying to accomplish. But we could not hope for advocacy from an assistant principal with whom we had failed to negotiate. The competing story was quickly turned into a conflicting story when moral symbols like exclusivity were associated with the way in which we functioned. My indignation solidified the transformation from competing to conflicting story. The complaint that a decision had already been reached was enough to suppress further discussion.

It is interesting for me to reflect now on how the decision was actually reached. When the staff claimed that a decision had already been reached, they talked about having reached a consensus, yet what actually had occurred was a vote. When I pointed this out my observations were quickly dismissed. No one seemed upset about the confusion of terms. Perhaps the distinction was unimportant at that point, when people were attempting to rid themselves of a conflicting story.

I wonder how we can begin to make space for multiple horizons of the sort that were, for a time, alive in our school. Can the dominant story and a competing one have some kind of parallel existence?

CHAPTER 11

A Story of Failed Professional Development

Janice Huber

"Debbie is having problems with classroom management. Do you think we could sit down with her this afternoon and talk about what you are doing in your classroom that is allowing you to not have discipline problems?" asked Paula, our principal.

Like me, Debbie was a first-year teacher. We were both teaching at the same grade level. A mixture of feelings moved through me as I looked at Paula. How would I feel if I were placed in Debbie's position rather than my own? Was there anything I could share that truly would be helpful? If I agreed to be part of this conversation, would my relationship with Debbie change? Even though I felt uncertain about the situation, I agreed to help in any way I could.

That afternoon, Debbie, Paula, and I met. I will never forget the sense of numbness I felt as I sat in Paula's office looking across at Debbie. She sat in her chair with her head hanging, tears dripping onto her hands, which she had clenched together on her lap. Paula reassured Debbie that she did not want her to feel that our conversation was any form of a reprimand. Rather, she wanted her to think of it as a sharing of ideas.

Paula continued by asking me to explain why I did not have discipline problems in my classroom. All I can remember saying was that I thought the children with whom I was working liked me, and because of this they monitored each other's behavior. She pressed me with further questions about how I had been able to create such an environment in my classroom. My sense of numbness grew stronger. Like a robot, I responded to her questions. Finally it was over. I got up from my chair, walked out of the office, put on my jacket, and walked home.

Debbie and I both worked at the school each evening. By the time I arrived back to the school on this particular evening, although I dreaded having to face her, I knew that I needed to say something. When I was finished working, I went down the darkened hallway to Debbie's room. She was seated at her desk on the opposite side of the classroom. Her eyes followed me as I moved closer, finally positioning myself on a nearby desk.

I told Debbie that I was embarrassed by what had happened that afternoon and that I felt I owed her an apology. Keeping her eyes downcast, she quietly said, "I do not want to talk about it." I wanted Debbie to know how confused I felt about what had happened. I explained that I felt angry for having allowed myself to participate in the conversation. I said that I did not think that I was a better teacher than she was. I told her how I never wanted to be placed into another situation like the one I had been in that afternoon. I explained how I felt as though the sense of trust I had been placing in Paula had been replaced with a sense of disillusionment. I said that because I felt this way, I had decided that, for the rest of the year, I would keep silent and keep myself as distant as possible from the rest of the staff. Debbie did not respond. The room was silent. I picked up my bag and left her classroom.

When I arrived at school the next morning, I found a note slipped under my door. It said:

> Dear Janice,
>
> Thanks for explaining our situation to me last night. I had thought we were becoming friends. I guess I was wrong.
>
> Debbie.

Since I have lived this story, I have always retold it in ways that spoke of my inability to make sense of why it happened or why I lived the story as I did. Although, even now, I cannot say that I entirely understand this story, I feel as though I have begun to make some sense of it. When I place this story within the context of this book, I am able to retell its events with new insights. I retell my story this way.

Each time I reflected on this story, I asked myself, "Why have I storied this conversation among Paula, Debbie, and I as hurtful and troubling rather than as a 'sharing of ideas'?"

As I thought about the professional knowledge landscape of this school, I paid close attention to the part lived by my principal, Paula. Paula had been both a teacher and an administrator for many years prior to the time Debbie and I joined her staff. Through numerous returnings on this story and other stories of my time in this school, I have come to recognize that an important thread in Paula's story as an educator was "working together." Paula continuously encouraged our staff to work with one another, with the children in our classrooms, with their parents, and with other teachers in the school district. Teachers at the same grade level often worked together to plan units; teachers from different grade levels worked together to plan school events; and teachers worked with parents to plan activities for the children and to raise money for certain school events. When I consider Paula's story of working together, I can make more sense of why she asked me to participate with her and Debbie in a conversation about classroom management. I believe she was working to create a space in which the three of us could share ideas about working with children in classrooms.

This, however, is where the events of my story require careful unraveling. Even though Paula intended our time together to be a positive growth experience, neither Debbie nor I storied it in this manner. I believe that Debbie tells the story of this afternoon as feeling inadequate and that she was being compared with me. In essence, she tells a story in which her knowing was not as "right" or as "good" as mine or Paula's.

In quite a similar way, I have told this story with anger. My anger stemmed from being frustrated with myself because I did not have the confidence to tell Paula that I did not want to participate in the conversation. My discomfort was, I believe, connected to the fact that she would evaluate my first year of teaching, an evaluation that I thought would have a tremendous shaping effect on my continuing career. I have also been angry with Paula because she obviously did not foresee the damage that a conversation such as this could cause.

A consideration of the character of our professional knowledge landscape, however, gives me insight as to why the events of this story were played out in the manner in which they were. Debbie and I were both beginning teachers—fresh recruits from university environments in which competition and isolation are consequences of the sacred theory-practice story. Prior to our living of this story, I did not sense that Debbie and I were constructing stories of having to compete with one another or of not valuing the tremendous sense of growth and of safety that occurs when people come together to share ideas. On the contrary, because Debbie was also a beginning teacher, teaching at the same grade level as I was, I valued the times when we sat in one another's classroom in the evenings and shared our wonders. It was through conversations such as these that we were coming to trust one another, to speak in authentic voices, and to share secret stories of ourselves.

After the events of our conversation concerning classroom management, however, our relationship changed. Not only did Debbie and I no longer visit each other's classroom in the evenings, but we seldom talked with one another. Our narratives of beginning teacher development became separate and isolated rather than narratives of collaboration and interconnection. I have often thought about the tremendous shaping effect this story had on the remainder of my time in this school. I also wonder about other beginning teachers who feel excited about working with, and learning from, their peers yet who come to the same sense of disconnection and mistrust that Debbie and I came to. I wonder if Paula did not foresee the damaging nature of this situation because she was more accustomed to working with teachers who, through time, had come to feel comfortable in the out-of-classroom places on their professional landscapes.

As I thought about this, I also wondered what it was about the differences in our teaching that caught Paula's attention in the first place. Had I been pressed, I probably would have said that Paula thought I was doing a better job. By agreeing to the conversation, I fell into this story. And, given that, Debbie's reaction was not surprising. As I pursue this further, I feel that it is not so much a matter of poorer and better teaching but that Debbie was seen as living a story of classroom management that was outside the horizon of what was acceptable in Paula's school. In this way of viewing the incident, I fit the school story of good management. While this telling of my story allows me to fit within the horizon of the school story, I do not want my story told as good classroom management, for this is not how I would define my relationship with the children with whom I worked. Rather, speaking of community more adequately captures the story the children and I lived each day in our classroom.

Close consideration of the nature of our professional knowledge landscape has given me much insight as to why the events of this story were played out in the manner in which they were and why I lived this story as I did. Thinking about trust, relationship, school stories and the landscape has been central to my unraveling of this story and to the new meanings I have made of the events of this story.

CHAPTER 12

Working with Subject Matter, Working with Students, Learning Stories of Control

Rosalie Young and Ming Fang He

Teresa Eastman, a first-year science teacher, was exhausted by January. She was working with grade-10, nonacademic, general-level students, a science curriculum that was structured and demanding, and a noisy classroom. This is a story of Teresa's attempt to live out an image of herself as a teacher who respects students at the same time that she respects the structure of the discipline of science and the curriculum guidelines that go with it. It is a story in which she receives support from other teachers and disapproval from the vice-principal, who sees her as having classroom management problems.

Teresa's experience as a high school and university science student convinced her to teach science in a structured way. The provincial curriculum guidelines, she thought, supported this view. In her attempts to live out this view, she reasoned that disciplined study habits based on a methodical system of student note taking were important. This teaching approach would, she believed, help her keep track of content delivery, provide a way to assign part of the course grade in a manner that rewarded diligent students for taking good notes while occupying disruptive students, and give students something to study. Other teaching strategies she adopted were writing text passages on the blackboard for students to copy, giving students organized equipment for science experiments, and using a system of demonstrating the correct steps in scientific experiments. She gave directions on how to write up experiments by identifying selective text excerpts and by requiring detailed information for each experiment organized under the headings of hypothesis, equipment, observation, and findings. For Teresa, these structured activities were consistent with her beliefs about science as a discipline and with the curriculum guidelines. The activities were also a way to keep students engaged with curriculum tasks. They were, as well, a way to maintain classroom control.

Teresa also thought that this method of teaching science would make it possible for her to work with students in a way that she believed was important. She was concerned for students as individuals and often spoke quietly with an individual student about his or her work during class. She was sensitive to each student and wanted to leave space and time for students to interact with her and with each other. She was inclined to accept student talk and noisy activity as a normal part of their learning.

How was this working? It wasn't. Her days were hell. She was frustrated in her attempts to interest students in the subject matter. She spent much of her time trying to maintain order, policing students and scolding them for not doing their homework. She wanted to ignore student talk and the disruptive noise during her lectures but felt her first job was to get her students' cooperation. She felt that unless students were cooperating with her she was not teaching but was only disciplining. Teresa was unhappy about her classroom. She wanted to teach—which, for her, meant working closely with individual students. But this was not what was happening. "I came to teaching to teach, not to discipline," she would say.

As Teresa searched for ways to improve her teaching, she turned to science and her working notions of how to teach it as the starting point to change things. She questioned the structured nature of the science program and its relevance to student lives. She put it this way:

> I feel that the structuredness of the high school science program has facilitated my first year of teaching but at the same time, I am beginning to see some of the disadvantages such a structured program has for science students. Science is supposed to be a process, but with such a structured program which dictates exactly which and how experiments are to be done, this process is gradually being masked. Structured versus unstructured science program. . . this will be my issue of concern. (Conversation, January 27, 1991)

It is clear that Teresa's reflections on the structure of the science program were framed in terms of her ongoing concern for students. With respect to the sequence of unit plans she said:

> Perhaps I should not work from unit to unit, finishing one before starting the other. But perhaps I should approach them with a discrepant event that triggers questions, and leads to hypotheses and experimental investigations designed by the students to answer their questions. But perhaps the one discrepant event does not interest all 30 students. Perhaps I could demonstrate five or more dis-

> crepant events. Have students choose the one they would like to investigate.
>
> This could incorporate some cooperative group work. These investigations might hopefully lead students to more questions that could be investigated. I wonder if this would be sufficient in covering the whole program. (Conversation, January 9, 1991)

In this excerpt, Teresa is searching for ways of planning her science teaching that go beyond the structure of subject matter and take student interests and learning preferences into account. She told her story of difficult classroom teaching in terms both of the structure of science and science teaching and in terms of student interest. The task, as she saw it, was to work out a workable resolution of these matters.

But this was not how Teresa's classroom was viewed by the vice-principal. The vice-principal described Teresa as having a discipline problem and her students as being out of control. Teresa was surprised at this response to her classroom. For her, control was not the issue. She was trying to figure out how to capture student interest and to cope with the various student demands on her time. Teresa's interest in trying to engage each child in learning meant that she had a different story of the classroom from that of the vice-principal. The vice-principal's concern about discipline expresses a common story of classroom management. It is a story in the out-of-classroom place often told by those outside of classrooms.

In other places in the out-of-classroom part of the landscape, Teresa felt lucky to be part of a supportive team. She was able to discuss her apprehensions and uncertainties with more experienced teachers, who responded positively and offered reassurance. Some offered their lesson plans and materials. She felt supported and encouraged by her fellow teachers and department head. These teachers' concern and support is different from that of the vice-principal and is embodied within a competing story of learning to teach. The one story has it that learning to control students is key to learning to teach; the other has it that learning to teach is learning what works from colleagues.

For Teresa, these different responses meant that the out-of-classroom part of the landscape was a place of competing advice. It was a place where the vice-principal, living one story, gave one kind of advice, and Teresa's colleagues, living another story, gave another kind of advice. But there seems to have been no place for Teresa to sort out the complex interweaving of what it means for her to be a science teacher.

CHAPTER 13

Competing and Conflicting Stories on the Landscape

D. Jean Clandinin and F. Michael Connelly

The previous three chapters offer stories of teachers living out their professional lives in three schools. The events in these chapters are small, everyday kinds of events—the sort of events that happen in teachers' lives all the time, wherever they teach. But the events are far from trivial for the professional lives of the teachers involved, and they are far from trivial in terms of what these stories tell about life on the out-of-classroom place on the professional knowledge landscape. These are stories of teachers negotiating their professional lives with their colleagues. There are serious, significant consequences for how these teachers know themselves as professionals.

REVISITING PAT'S STORY

To situate readers, we need to provide a brief sketch of Hogan's chapter. Pat Hogan came to the school in question at the beginning of the principal's second year. During the principal's first year, she learned of an innovation in professional development: differentiated professional development. In the principal's second year, Pat's first year at the school, she introduced this notion and the staff divided into three professional-development groups. Pat and her team partner Stacey joined one group. This group became confident enough with each other to write journals, which they shared, and to begin to tell one another secret classroom teaching stories. At the start of Pat's second year, this group was brought into question by members of the other groups and by a new assistant principal. All three groups were eventually disbanded.

As we tried to understand this story in terms of the professional knowledge landscape, we began by realizing that the push for differentiated professional development came via the conduit. The principal learned about it from a presentation outside the school. As we interpret events, the principal, Pat, Stacey, and perhaps other teachers as well, saw this as a significant new way to engage in professional development, perhaps even a way to challenge the sacred theory-practice story as it ordinarily unfolds in professional development. Instead of relying on experts in the system or elsewhere, they were called on to rely on their own resources. This is a fundamental change in professional development and, if acted on, is a competing story to the sacred story of professional development.

The sense that these groups were more than just another way of doing professional development but were, instead, representative of a new sense of what it means to be professional is evident in the doubts and sense of unease created among other staff members in the school. Pat and Stacey became aware that others were somewhat suspicious of what they were doing. On the face of it, there is no particular reason for this because nothing was being done in a competitive way that would either interfere with the work of the other two groups or alter anyone's classroom teaching. As one looks at the events described by Hogan, one wonders why anyone would mind what Pat's group was doing. After all, the group did not impinge on anyone else, either individually or collectively, in their classrooms or out of them, nor did it put them at any competitive advantage with respect to assignments and promotion. Why were other teachers so concerned? Our answer is that their concerns grew out of a vague sense of unease that the world on their school landscape was not unfolding as it should. It was not a matter of the teachers' feeling negatively influenced by Pat and Stacey's group; it was a matter of feeling that Pat and Stacey's group was acting out of character. Its actions were incompatible with the sacred story within which people established their professional identity.

What does the sacred story applied to professional development look like? In Chapter 6, we wrote that teachers have been taught that they have incomplete knowledge and that they will have to continue to learn through returning to the university for professional development. Experts, of course, reside not only in the university; they reside in other schools, in central board offices, and in other places. The professional-development story, embedded in the sacred theory-practice story, is, then, one in which teachers have incomplete knowledge. Furthermore, they are not knowers who can teach one another; they are learners to be taught by experts. Thus, professional development conducted in terms of the sacred theory-practice story has teachers returning to the university; attending professional development day workshops led by university people or, perhaps, by master teachers, principals, mentor teachers, consultants, coordinators, or superintendents who have studied whatever is being promoted in the professional development; reading articles, books, policies, and curriculum documents on the advice of, and often on the requirement of, someone in the conduit; and otherwise doing the many things that are visited on teachers in the name of professional development.

Let us imagine what went on in Pat and Stacey's small group by way of contrast to the above. There were, we imagine, wine, dinners, journal exchanges, and the reading of research books written by researchers who interested group members. We imagine that specific stories of classroom teaching were told and retold and we imagine that the difficulties captured in the stories were softened by laughter. No wonder there was suspicion. Professional development, according to the sacred story, is not an occasion for enjoyment; it is serious business. It is not an occasion for informal activities in personal settings, but a time for formal activities in professional settings.

Pat saw her group as increasingly gaining control of what she called "real talk." This was talk about things that actually happened and things that actually mattered in the day-to-day life on both places on the professional knowledge landscape. There was, we imagine, little abstraction and nothing in the way of a rhetoric of conclusions in the talk that increasingly took place in this group. It was not only the teachers in the other two groups that were worried. Members of Pat and Stacey's group were also worried, as evidenced in their feelings of guilt. Presumably they thought they were enjoying themselves too much and were too connected to the specifics of their ongoing experiences in their professional lives. Professional development is rarely the way we imagine it to have been in their group. It is almost always something theoretical, something abstract, something at a distance to "take back to your school" to be applied. What they talked about was not to be applied; rather, it was reflection on what they were doing.

The stories told in Pat and Stacey's group were secret stories, stories not usually made public. For Pat and Stacey, the group amounted to a safe place for the telling of secret stories. Pat and Stacey were trying to create the kind of place we spoke about in the last part of Chapter 1. This story of making secret stories into public ones reverberates with the stories of Chapters 2 and 3, where we laid out the idea of a matrix of relationships in which personal, public, and secret stories are related. For example, in Chapter 3, we say "In the sacred story of theory-practice relationships the quality of the relationships among the in-classroom place on the professional knowledge landscape the out-of-classroom place on the professional knowledge landscape, and the personal knowledge landscape, is given by the conduit. It may be given in one form, taken away, and formed anew." This notion of the matrix of relationships gives us a way to think about how the professional-development activity was experienced by others in the school. We want to think first about the unease of other teachers in Pat and Stacey's group as an unease born of an embodied sense that the matrix of relationships was altered by what was going on in their group. They knew that the sacred story given by the conduit turned the telling of classroom stories into the telling of "war stories" and acts of gossip. In fact, at one point, people worried about the group degenerating into little more than "bitch sessions." Since, however, authorities in the conduit, specifically the principal, had warranted what Pat and Stacey's group was doing, why would this worry exist? The answer is that if told from within the sacred story, as it was, the sessions could only be seen as bitch sessions.

We want to bring forward to this discussion a consideration of the moral quality of life on the professional knowledge landscape. The guilty feelings of other members in Pat and Stacey's group, and the eventual criticism leveled at the group by members of the other two groups, were moral. As Hogan told her story, she spoke of the other groups' charges of "jealousy," "cliques," and "exclusivity." These terms all convey a moral tone, suggesting that people are not acting properly with respect to one another. This moralizing seems odd and out of place when the bare account of what the group was doing is considered. But that account, placed in the matrix of relationships set within the sacred theory-practice story, is readily explicable. The guilt that some members felt, and the moral accusations that others leveled, may be seen as direct consequences of the immoral quality of Pat and Stacey's group's activities judged against the horizons of what is proper as specified by the sacred story.

We further believe, as we said in Chapter 3, that the teachers who raised questions about Pat and Stacey's group sensed that what was given by the conduit could just as easily be taken away—as, indeed, it eventually was. In effect, this form of professional development was not, in the end, under the teachers' control and auspices. It flourished, while it did, because of being sanctioned by the sacred story.

The sacred story embedded in Hogan's account is harder to see, and is subtler to uncover, than is the sacred story embedded in curriculum implementation and policy initiatives disseminated through school systems. There is nothing subtle about such activities. They are clearly designed by some to change the behavior of others. The various mechanisms of the conduit are well designed to deliver their content to the professional knowledge landscape, thereby bending teachers to new forms of knowledge and to new codes of conduct. But the case described by Hogan happens, for all intents and purposes, on the landscape at the other end of the conduit. It happens by and among teachers, not to teachers. What happens is not so much the simple application of power and authority relations that commonly characterize curriculum implementation and policy initiatives. Rather, it is a matter of participants' personal practical knowledge shaped by the conduit. It is a matter of people's biographies and how they are living out their professional lives. These are professionals who, at least on the out-of-classroom place on the professional knowledge landscape, have embodied the sacred theory-practice story. They live this story and their professional identity is given by it. That is the central dilemma of Chapter 1 and it is the dilemma that makes the story so painful for Pat. She is exploring options, an alternative story. She believes that she and her colleagues can start and live out a competing story on the landscape. But she learns the lesson that the moral quality of her professional life is neither in her hands nor in those of a sympathetic principal. Rather, she learns that the moral quality of her professional life is in the story that permeates and pervades the professional knowledge landscape. She is not up against recalcitrant teachers or a recalcitrant principal. She is up against a sacred story of theory and practice. In the eventual conflict that becomes apparent on her school's landscape, that story wins.

REVISITING JANICE'S STORY

We begin by providing a brief sketch of Huber's chapter. As we read it, we learn that two beginning teachers, Janice and Debbie, have been learning to trust each other as people who could share secret stories of teaching in the safety of their relationship. They had learned to count on their relationship as a place to tell and retell their stories of teaching. Their principal, believing that she could improve Debbie's classroom management skills, asks Janice to tell Debbie how Janice manages her class. The principal invokes the expert story, saying that Janice has good classroom management, and uses her to act as expert. As in Hogan's account, there are sad consequences. Putting Janice in the role of expert relative to Debbie dramatically reshaped their relationship to one more common on the landscape. Janice and Debbie became distrustful not only of the principal but of each other. They learned to live cover stories on the out-of-classroom place on the professional knowledge landscape.

Janice blames the unhappy situation on herself. She feels that if she had been more experienced, more confident, had trusted her feelings more, she could have resisted the principal's plan. She could have refused to be named expert knower in relation to Debbie. The fault, as she sees it, was firmly situated in how she responded to the principal who was, after all, living a story of "working together," a story Janice found appealing. It was how the principal's story of working together was lived out on the landscape, and the expert character Janice was required to play vis-à-vis her friend and colleague, Debbie, that concerned Janice. Huber tells the story as one that could have succeeded if she had broken out of her biography and had helped her principal break free of hers. The story then might have been different. Janice could, she thinks, have reshaped the landscape.

REVISITING TERESA'S STORY

Teresa is a beginning teacher who comes to science teaching with an image of science as a discipline and an idea of how it should be taught and an image of children and how a teacher should relate to them. She sees science as a structured discipline to be taught in a structured way and she sees children as active learners with whom teachers should establish personal relationships. When she begins teaching she experiences difficulty. On the out-of-classroom part of the landscape, she receives competing advice from a vice-principal who tells her that she needs to develop better classroom management and teaching colleagues who provide her with ready-made lessons and other items of practical advice. Teresa, however, is trying to restory her images of teaching and looks to people on the out-of-classroom place with whom to do this. However, she is left alone with no one but the project researchers to work through her difficult teaching situation in her own terms.

In this retelling, we see that the character Teresa is required to live does not fit well with her sense of identity. Through conversations with the researchers she tries to rethink her professional identity and to work out a new, livable story.

ORIGINS OF THE COMPETING STORIES

One of the striking differences among the three chapters is in the origin of the competing stories told. The competing story of professional development in Hogan's chapter originates in the conduit, with the principal. The sense of this story's belonging to the teachers comes after its introduction to the school. Pat and Stacey make a conscious effort to keep this story alive as a competing story of professional development.

The competing story of professional development in Huber's chapter develops and is nurtured spontaneously as the two novice teachers, Janice and Debbie, turn to one another for reflective support. As novice teachers, they were unaware of what was expected on the out-of-classroom place on the professional knowledge landscape. To return to our matrix notion, these two teachers began to build bridges across the personal and professional and across the in-classroom and out-of-classroom places on the professional knowledge landscape. They were constructing a landscape that would have been familiar to Marion Connelly of Chapter 3. They spent a large part of their private time in the school and it became a kind of home for them as they returned to work every evening and as they worked on weekends and shared accounts of their teaching lives.

There is a sense of innocence about the competing story being constructed by their relationship. There is no sense, as there was in Hogan's chapter, of teachers doing anything special or different. They were simply doing what young people in a new, challenging, professional setting might do when left to their own devices. What they missed was that what they were doing was not only up to their own devices. Their actions could well have been read by other teachers in a way similar to the reading of Pat and Stacey's group by teachers in the other two groups. Other teachers might well have charged Janice and Debbie with exclusivity. Indeed, teachers probably did ask questions about what Janice and Debbie did in the school at night and on weekends. But it was not other teachers' questions that awakened Janice. It was a well-intentioned initiative by the principal to help Debbie improve her teaching by drawing on the resources of Janice that awakened Janice and made clear to her the sense in which it was the matrix that gave permission for the moral quality of her relationship with Debbie. This was our point in Chapter 3 when we said that modern-day teachers may act in ways that are similar to teachers from Marion Connelly's day but that their actions are given moral authority not by the teachers but by their place in the matrix.

The principal's intervention awakened Janice to the stories lived out on the professional knowledge landscape. Indeed, Janice goes beyond her feelings of anger at losing a friend to disbelief that her story of working with children had been read by her principal in the familiar professional knowledge landscape language of classroom management. Janice has, in effect, awakened to the landscape. We can imagine that she will now know that her personal practical knowledge of teaching is always set in a context of professional knowledge on the landscape. She has lost her innocence about the relationship of her personal practical knowledge of teaching and its context on the professional knowledge landscape.

The competing story of professional development for Teresa originates, as did Janice and Debbie's, in her desire for a place to learn to cope with her two images of teaching. A professional-development story emerges when, on the one hand, Teresa is told by the vice-principal to control her students through firmer discipline and, on the other hand, teacher colleagues provide her with ready-made materials and exercises. She is concerned at the vice principal's advice because she does not want to control her students through firmer discipline but wants their cooperation and she is pleased at the help the other teachers give her. But she is left with no place to live out a story of professional development that would allow her to tell her secret stories of classroom teaching. She is strongly motivated to create a retold story of teaching but finds that the out-of-classroom place on the landscape gives her help only in the language of the conduit. People advise her on what to do. As with Janice and Debbie, there is a sense of innocence about the competing story she desires. She has no real sense that the landscape might, under a different story, have provided a place for self-reflection. As the story is told, Teresa is not yet aware of the relationship of her personal practical knowledge and its context on the professional knowledge landscape.

SUMMARY

As we look back over the three chapters, and revisit the three stories, we note that Pat's story ends with a sense that the unfolding of the professional-development story is more than a question of biography. It is also a question of the landscape. Pat appears to believe that those involved with the competing story—the principal, Stacey, and herself—had restoried their biographies. But this was not enough. The moral horizons of the landscape were given by the sacred theory-practice story. In order to keep the competing story alive she and her colleagues had to change the landscape, a virtually impossible task for a small group of teachers. Janice's story, however, ends with a sense that had she restoried her own biography, she would have kept alive her competing stories of relationship on the landscape. For Janice, the problem with sustaining competing stories was with individual teacher's stories. She has less of a sense, at least as told in Chapter 11, than does Pat that competing stories are turned into conflicting ones and silenced by the sacred theory-practice story. Teresa, as the story is told, is not yet aware that she is trying to live a competing story of professional development.

Perhaps both Janice and Pat looked back on their stories and wondered what happened. They noticed that people and events went on. They may take nostalgic looks back on their competing stories and the promise that they held and wonder what happened to them. What Hogan, Huber, Young, and He have done by calling these stories forward and naming them allows us to see what happens to competing stories that hold promise for change on the landscape.

PART V

SAFE PLACES ON THE PROFESSIONAL KNOWLEDGE LANDSCAPE

CHAPTER 14

Safe Places on the Professional Knowledge Landscape: Knowledge Communities

Cheryl Craig

In our collaborative work, Tim and Benita both considered the conversational spaces we created for ourselves "safe places" (Conversations, Tim, July 9, 1991; Benita, November 10, 1991) on the professional knowledge landscape. I realized that what they called safe places were what I call knowledge communities (Craig, 1992). In this chapter, I describe the spaces that Tim and Benita found to be safe places on their professional knowledge landscapes. I illustrate qualities of these places, these knowledge communities, by highlighting particular aspects of Tim's and Benita's stories. I also explore the promise that knowledge communities hold as sanctuaries on teachers' landscapes.

QUALITIES OF KNOWLEDGE COMMUNITIES

In Chapters 7 and 8, Benita's good teaching image and Tim's healthy-school story were presented. Tim and Benita made sense of their teaching practices with a number of different people on their in-classroom and out-of-classroom places. Some of these people were on their school staffs; some were students, some were associated with the university, and some were family members. These people with whom Tim and Benita storied and restoried their first-year teaching experiences formed their knowledge communities.

People joined Tim's and Benita's knowledge communities through an originating event (Schein, 1985), that is, a common experience that brought them together in meaning. For example, Tim and Jonas came together because of their shared interest in sports and activities. The opportunity to share stories about their teaching experiences brought Annie and Benita into community with each other.

Tim and Benita needed to continue to negotiate these safe places, their communities. An example of a breakdown in a knowledge community is found in Tim's story. Dolores, a staff member, does not remain part of Tim's community in his second year of teaching. At first Dolores helped Tim feel accepted. She shared her knowledge with him and introduced him to "unwritten kinds of things" (Conversation, November 14, 1991) about the "school culture" (Conversation, July 9, 1991). Gradually Tim came to know the topography of the school landscape through the help of Dolores. But Dolores began to do things with which Tim did not morally agree. For example, she criticized Tim's organization of students in the classroom. While Tim believed the students needed to be in groups so they could talk to learn, Dolores believed they needed to be in straight rows so they could be quiet and learn. Tim also noted Dolores' "less positive" remarks in staff meetings. He did not agree with Dolores' beliefs about classroom management or with the way she presented herself in the school context. Tim sensed his association with Dolores could affect his relationship with other teachers and he felt the need "to pull away" (Conversation, July 8, 1991). Her responses made him feel it would be unsafe to continue to share his stories.

Tim's and Benita's knowledge communities also expanded to include new people. I joined both of their communities through our mutual acquaintances, Jean, Pat, and Annie. Because Tim and Benita trusted them, they thought they could trust me. Relationships with me would also provide safe places. Tim noted the similarity between Jean's and my responses to his work and said "I knew you would respond in this way. Jean always gave me responses like this" (Conversation, November 8, 1990).

Tim and Benita shared their stories with the people in their knowledge communities and these people offered them response. For example, when Tim initially figured out it was not safe for him to share his opinions in his school, he talked with me about the healthy-school story in the safety of our relationship. In return, I offered response. I tried to give the experiences back in ways that would help Tim and Benita safely explore new possibilities to live by.

Tim and Benita both created new knowledge for themselves in their conversations in community. Tim came to know the leadership story as he worked alongside Jonas, the vice-principal, preparing for Sports Day, and Benita developed a language to describe one of her substitute-teaching experiences as she told stories to Annie and me. When Benita served as a substitute teacher for students with learning disabilities, she expected a challenging experience. Unexpectedly, Benita found the day "easy" because the teacher had everything well prepared. Annie called Benita's experience a "safe day." A "safe day" became part of Benita's knowledge and part of our three-way conversations (Craig, Dalton, & Davies, 1992).

Tim and Benita told different versions of their stories in different knowledge communities. For example, as Tim lived the healthy-school story, he shared a sports and activities version of the story with Jonas while simultaneously sharing a story of concern about the number of activities with me. While Jonas encouraged Tim to become involved in more activities, I encouraged Tim to consider the effect his participation in activities was having on his teaching. Tim was sharing different versions of stories and getting different responses to them from different members of his knowledge communities.

In their knowledge communities, Tim and Benita linked their personal practical knowledge with their experiences in different places on the landscape. We see an example when Benita storied and restoried her notion of a "safe day" in community with Annie and me. When Benita first embraced the idea of a safe day, she approached it from a personal viewpoint. But as she told her stories to Annie and me, her knowledge of her landscape shifted and she extended the notion of safety to include all people in the situation, not just the teacher.

Because Tim and Benita met people in their knowledge communities over time, those people provided continuity in their reflections. They developed a language and ongoing themes that made it possible to construct connections among apparently dissimilar experiences. Even though there were many fragments emerging from Tim's and Benita's experiences in their professional knowledge landscapes, through talking in knowledge communities, they were able to bring some sense of unity to what they knew about themselves.

When Tim and Benita turned to their knowledge communities, they were not only negotiating meaning, they were also learning about the moral horizons of their professional knowledge landscapes. In safety, Tim and Benita shared stories that were outside the range of acceptable stories shared in other places on the landscape. Benita felt safe to tell Annie and me stories about her job uncertainties. Tim shared his concerns about school activities. Through their questioning and revisiting uncomfortable topics, the storying and restorying process unfolded. Unnoticed moral horizons came into view.

In the examples shared, Tim's and Benita's knowledge communities acted as moral bridges that helped them connect their personal practical knowledge with what they had come to know about their professional knowledge landscapes. The plots of the stories Tim and Benita told to members of their knowledge communities linked what they knew with what they were experiencing on their professional knowledge landscapes. In their knowledge communities, Tim and Benita linked their individual ways of knowing with communal ways of knowing the landscape. In safe places, Tim's and Benita's knowledge became public and shared just as the members of their knowledge communities made their knowledge public and shared (Dewey, 1916). Tim's and Benita's interpretations became fuller and more informed because their restorying of experiences in the security of particular relationships introduced them to multiple ways of knowing school situations. And Tim's and Benita's horizons of knowing merged with the horizons of knowing of their community members. Tim's and Benita's knowledge constructions and reconstructions were influenced by members of their knowledge communities but were not reducible to those of any one member.

What makes Benita's and Tim's knowledge communities markedly different from other places on their professional knowledge landscapes is that they were not dependent on, or driven by, the conduit. The relationships between people like Annie and Benita did not arise from the hierarchy of knowledge or the hierarchy of position. It was "the commonplaces of human experiences" (Lane, 1988, p. 15) which set their horizons and bound them together, not their relationship to one another as they lived out the sacred theory-practice story.

As described then, knowledge communities are relational places dotted on the professional knowledge landscape, safe places found outside the line of authority in schools and often outside of schools themselves. They are safe havens of the kind to which Tim and Benita turned when uneasiness and tension marked their knowing. In one way, Tim's and Benita's professional knowledge landscapes presented them with struggles and uncertainty. Yet, in another way, their knowledge communities situated on those landscapes offered them safe places for instruction and growth. Having described the qualities of knowledge communities, I turn now to discuss the promises they offer.

THE PROMISE OF KNOWLEDGE COMMUNITIES

What is the promise of knowledge communities? What makes knowledge communities important features to consider as we look at the complexity of teachers' relationships on their professional knowledge landscapes?

One significant feature of knowledge communities is that they are places where educators are vibrantly present, where their voices are unconditionally heard, where their relationships are authentic and secure. The dialectic between the individual teacher and the community of educators is nurtured. We see individuals like Tim, Benita, Annie, Pat, Jean, and myself becoming fuller human beings through our participation in community. We see knowledge communities becoming richer because of our individual contributions. Knowledge communities recognize and value teachers' personal practical knowledge and connect individuals to the communal ways of knowing.

Knowledge communities are also critical to our discussion of the professional knowledge landscape because they are seeding grounds for competing stories, stories that may lead to educational change. Knowledge communities promote this kind of growth. They are important during times of transition. Without the security that Tim's and Benita's knowledge communities offered, imagine how lonely and disconnected these beginning teachers would have been. Their knowledge communities became bridges for them in their matrixes of relationships: bridges among and between individuals, and bridges between small groups and large groups in their many places on the professional knowledge landscape. Their knowledge communities also were bridges between theory and practice—safe places where Tim and Benita found middle ground.

Knowledge communities are also important because they take the current emphasis away from schools as the sole units of educational change. Chapter 8's account of Tim's beginning teaching experiences particularly illustrates how counterproductive a singular emphasis on schools as sites of change can be. What was being promoted in the name of health in Tim's school was making the people and the institution unhealthy.

Knowledge communities emerge and grow as teachers come together in their professional knowledge landscapes. They cannot be imposed or mandated. They involve people from different places in the matrix of relationships on the landscape.

Throughout this chapter, I have emphasized other educators in out-of-classroom and out-of-school places who were part of Tim's and Benita's knowledge communities. Other knowledge communities are found in student-teacher relationships. Teachers create these safe places in and out of classrooms.

CHAPTER 15

Knowledge Communities in the Classroom

Janice Huber and Karen Whelan

Many stories come to mind as I think of Karen and the year I spent as a participant observer learning with her and the children in her classroom. As I reflect on these stories, images of Karen are strong in my mind—I see Karen's warm smile as she listens to the conversation of three children sharing wonders about how a caterpillar becomes a butterfly; I hear her laughter as a small group of children take puppets off the shelf and share a skit they have written after collaboratively reading *The Giving Tree* (Silverstein, 1964); I hear her voice softly encourage a child who is struggling as she tries to represent a number in expanded form using dienes blocks; I see the tears form in Karen's eyes and slowly begin to run down her cheeks as she listens to a child respond to *The Velveteen Rabbit* (Williams, 1981) by sharing his own story of how he became "real" when his Grandfather died. I can hear her speak to me about her work as a teacher and her relationships with children, colleagues, and parents.

I read through our shared journal, stopping here and there to reflect on our thoughts. I smile as I read Karen's response to one of my thoughts, at the end of which she wrote:

> The children and the flowers
> Like the colors of the rainbow
> Are a promise
> For tomorrow
> And a blessing for today.
> (Jody Bergsma, Journal Entry, p. 13)

I begin to think about how I came to know Karen's love for children and I realize how it seems only fitting that if I am to reconstruct Karen's stories, I should begin with children. For, in Karen's words, "Children are at the heart of what it means to me to be a teacher" (Journal Entry, p. 3).

As I reconstruct one story of Karen and how she works with the children in her classroom to create a safe, caring classroom, I cannot tell it without telling other stories. As Metzger (1986) writes, "Stories go in circles. They don't go in straight lines. So it helps if you listen in circles because there are stories inside stories and stories between stories" (p. 104). As the reader of this chapter, it is important that you, too, read in circles.

SAFE PLACES IN THE CLASSROOM

One story that Karen frequently tells is her story of Jason. Karen worked with Jason during her teacher education practicum. As she tells the story, Jason influenced her development as a teacher. In the following, I illustrate this by interweaving two texts, Karen's written story of Jason, which she named "The Dove," and a transcript of a conversation between Karen and me.

> The reason I always come back to Jason is because he was one of my first stories. He was a child from my student teaching. . . . Well he was in my . . . practicum and he was a real misfit. Like he was one of those kids that everybody else picked on . . . as soon as I came into the school there were stories about Jason. As soon as I entered the classroom kids were coming up to me and saying "Watch out for Jason, he has a bad temper and he's mean" and Rose, my cooperating teacher, told me he was seeing a psychologist and psychiatrist and he had a volatile temper and he could explode at any moment and so I had him labeled right away. I was on him all the time and the thing about Jason, though, was he was a really neat kid.
>
> He always wore a black leather jacket. Even if it was sweltering. Like this was in May and June. He wore a black leather jacket every day. He had big black thick glasses. Short greasy hair that he kind of slicked to the side and his jeans were always a little bit too short. He was from a broken home and he was just a little waif and he was just a tiny kid but with a big mouth. . . . Like he could get himself into trouble. Like he'd go lip off some boys and then he'd be too tiny to do anything about it. But the experience of Jason stayed with me.
>
> It was an experience I recognized right away at the time because this experience moved me to tears . . . I was really upset about it and it caused me to go back a year later and visit that kid and see if he was okay because I really did do him an injustice. You know, we talk about humanizing and dehumanizing kids and I did

> dehumanize that boy that day and I don't think I've ever done it again to another kid . . . it had to happen that one time for me to know it.
>
> What happened was we went to the art room and I was in there by myself with the kids and they had been working all day on this dough art and they were in painting their dough art. . . . I was washing and my back was turned and I hear this slap and I turn around and there was this little Rebecca who was like a Miss Prim and Proper type of kid . . . Jason had slapped her across the face and there was a big red handmark on her face and everything and I just reacted. I didn't think or anything, I just went over and that afternoon we were having a Hawaiian dance. The class had been doing this theme on Hawaii and we had food and dancing and limbo and all that kind of stuff and Jason had been talking about that thing for weeks. He had taped music for it, he had picked out his outfit and he missed out on that because of that incident. . . .
>
> It was Rose's decision that he not come and do you know where he sat the whole time? Down the hallway and outside the office all the afternoon where the music was playing and everything and do you know what I found out later? This isn't even the crusher yet. What happened was he had made a dove for his mom, that's why I call the story "The Dove," and Rebecca said it looked like a turkey. . . . So he hit her. So who was more in the wrong?
>
> And if I hadn't have reacted to that situation I could have brought it right down. Because see I acted and I yelled at him. I can remember what I said to him. I said, "You're going to miss out on the Hawaiian party for this one mister" and I grabbed him by the arm. . . . He was so angry that he left the room and I went over and consoled Rebecca and really she should have missed out too.
>
> And his friend didn't participate in the afternoon. He was really upset that Jason couldn't. . . . Jason had left a note for Rose and I in our plan book apologizing for his behavior. (Conversation, May 17, 1992)

Karen continued to share her story of Jason by reading excerpts from "The Dove," which she wrote five years ago in an undergraduate reflective journal. She read the following from her journal:

> I will never forget this incident because I know how much it hurt Jason. In reflecting back on it I know that Rebecca's words were far more painful to Jason than a slap was to her face. After I reacted in

> the situation I immediately regretted my actions. I hadn't taken the time to really find out what had gone on and as a result, Jason missed out on an activity he was so looking forward to. I learned a very valuable lesson that day. I have to closely monitor the effect my actions will have on a child at an emotional level. It bothers me so much that I only saw and reacted to the physical slap. The damage Rebecca's words had caused went unnoticed until later, when it was too late to repair the damage that was done. To make things worse Jason left me a note in my plan book apologizing for his behavior. The next day I had told Jason that I had felt badly about how I had reacted and that it was wrong for Rebecca to criticize his art work. I know this didn't help much. Especially since he had missed the party and Rebecca hadn't. I guess it made me realize that . . . I will inevitably make mistakes with children. (Conversation, May 17, 1992)

I tell this story as one of awakening, an experience that caused Karen to reflect on her beliefs about children and her interactions with them. Through reflection on her experience with Jason, Karen began to develop a personal creed for her teaching. Karen describes her personal creed thus:

> I believe in honoring human potential . . . meaning that everyone has a place that they can move to. . . . I believe in providing a safe, nurturing environment where children are free to explore their own gifts. . . . I liken myself to a gardener because I believe that every flower in the garden can bloom . . . it's the idea that provided with the right care, with the right environment, every child can blossom. . . . I believe in laughter in the classroom and love and friendship. I believe in trust because I think it's the foundation for meaningful relationships. . . . I believe in faith, hope, and happiness as guiding forces in my life. . . . By faith I mean faith in God too and hope . . . I believe in the continuous process of becoming. (Conversation, May 17, 1992)

Karen's personal creed has evolved and is a strong foundation from which she works with the children in her classroom.

As I worked with Karen that year, I came to see the "stories inside stories and stories between stories" that make up a network of stories of Karen learning from children. Karen works closely with her children, watching for telling moments in their development and interactions with one another. The following excerpts from our conversations are examples of two such stories.

> . . . even with *Animalia,* Grahame Base's book, I read that book three times and I was reading it with Pat and I said, "What do you notice about the letters? What do you notice about the page?" and Pat said, "Well like on 'C,'" everything in the picture starts with 'C.'" I said, "What do you mean?" and he said, "Well look, there's a cat, a castle, a card." I didn't even notice that before! And if I didn't notice it there were probably children who also did not notice it. I read the book three times and I didn't notice that . . . I was looking at it from one point of view and that child helped me see the other side of it. (Conversation, January 26, 1992)

As Karen and I were discussing the support the children give each other in the classroom, Karen told a second story about how the children supported a child with special needs.

> You know where I really see it though? I really see it with Lila. I watched those kids, Alexandra, Shawn, and Lila working the other day. . . . I was watching them work together and they were just letting Lila color all over that cover. They weren't saying, "Well Lila why don't you color this in?" I would even be tempted to do that myself. I would be tempted to draw the picture and have her color it because she colors really well and she likes doing that but they were just, well they asked her to draw a flower and she drew a flower with little petals and everything, the first time I have ever seen her do something like that and I thought to myself if those kids hadn't let her draw a flower I may never have seen that she can draw a flower. They were just so supportive of her. She drew those patches all over their cover and they just let her and . . . I wasn't there supervising, I just came around and that's what I saw and I thought, "That's where you really see their acceptance of other children, especially those with special needs." (Conversation, January 26, 1992)

As Karen reflects on these and similar events, her practices change. She wants to make an environment that nurtures each individual child and she works hard to transform the physical space of the classroom into a warm, stimulating, learning environment. There are large-group, small-group and individual spaces for learning. There are spaces for reading, for writing, for painting, and for problem solving.

I remember my first visit to the classroom and how it was the brilliance of color that invited me inside. All the colors of the rainbow were represented on the walls, bookshelves, and displays in the classroom. I read messages like "Welcome," "Love," "Hugs Given Here," "Together Is a Wonderful Place to Be," "Together We Are Strong," and "Kids Are Special." I was intrigued by the puppets and how Karen had hundreds of books in baskets, on bookshelves, and arranged in special places throughout the classroom. I also noted that there was no teacher's desk.

Karen's construction of the physical space, however, is only the beginning. Rather than spending the month of September testing to determine where each child is in his or her learning, Karen uses this month to work with the children to build the foundation for a collaborative community to be lived in the classroom. Karen's thoughts about the importance of establishing a shared sense of classroom ownership is highlighted in the following excerpt from our conversation:

> *Janice:* Karen, don't you think that some of the things that really bring that together, like the community that exists here, is created by the value you place on the children sharing and by giving them voice? I think they realize this is their community, it's not your community that you have built for them.
>
> *Karen:* It's our community. I really believe that. I don't believe that it is just the kids. I think, obviously to me, the kids are the most important part of it but I really do see the room as our room. I live here too. I live here every day and it is important for me that I feel comfortable here and the kids live here everyday . . . I think that the things I do, the conscious decisions I make are for the children. (Conversation, September 23, 1991)

It is not only the physical space of the classroom or the beginning of the school year that tells a story of Karen and the children being in community with one another. The relationships in the classroom community are continually nurtured. Karen gives one example in the following passage:

> Because of what I am doing in the classroom the children are picking up on that and internalizing it and it kind of struck me when we were talking about teachers as leaders in the classroom in this course. The whole idea of the significant models we are for kids. Like even when we share our stories with kids or are sitting there trying to make sense of experiences. Like when I talk about the things that I am afraid of in the dark and when kids see teachers themselves trying to make sense. (Conversation, October 19, 1991)

When the children see Karen also trying to make sense of her experience, she sees it as contributing to the sense of trust and safety in their classroom community.

Karen also works within the classroom community to help the children accept and celebrate individual differences. For example, the celebration of each person's special gifts began one morning in this way:

> Karen brought the children back to the cozy corner and they shared *Frederick* (Lionni, 1967). This story tells of a mouse named Frederick. Frederick, however, is not like other mice as he does not prepare for winter in the same manner as they do.
>
> When the other mice question Frederick about this, he tells them that he is gathering sun rays to warm the cold dark winter days; colors to brighten the grayness of winter; and words, as the winter days are long and many and the mice will run out of things to say. Before long the supplies gathered by the other mice have run out and they are reminded of the supplies Frederick had gathered. The mice remind Frederick of his supplies, which he shares with them. As Frederick spoke to the mice of the sun, they began to feel warmer; when Frederick talked of color, he helped the other mice see pictures of colors that they had painted in their minds; and when Frederick shared his words with them, he helped the other mice experience poetry.
>
> After this story was shared, Karen and the children discussed what Frederick's special gift was. Karen asked the children to spend some time thinking about what their special gifts were. The children talked in their groups and drew pictures of their gifts. Some of the children had time to begin writing in their memoir about their special gifts and why they chose to represent the gift that they did.
>
> The gifts that the children represented are hung above the corridor of windows on one of the lengthwise walls of the classroom. After the gifts were hung, Karen and the children talked about what kind of a special message they should put below the pictures. Elsa suggested: "When We Live Together, Love Lives with Us." The class voted unanimously that they wanted this message displayed below their gifts. (Field notes, September 9, 1991)

Through my participation in the classroom, I also lived this story with Karen and the children. Each day there was an ongoing recognition that each person in the classroom was a unique person; we were different from one another and it was these unique qualities that made each one of us special.

Such an acceptance of individuality is restoried throughout each day in a variety of ways. For example, support circle was a special time in the classroom when everyone gathered into a large circle in the cozy corner to support one another as they wondered together and shared and explored their own and others' stories. I wrote the following story after a support-circle experience during which I felt moved by what I saw happening between the children:

> During the support circle this afternoon, Jessica shared her story of how she sleeps with a teddy bear. Before Jessica shared her story, however, we talked about how she wanted to share but was afraid to. Together, as a group, we spent time talking about how we wanted the support circle to feel safe and supportive and how we did not want anyone to feel uncomfortable sharing their stories.
>
> The room was completely still for many minutes after Jessica shared her story. It was wonderful how a number of the other children responded to her story and supported her by telling her how she should not feel afraid about telling them that she sleeps with a teddy bear. The realness and honesty of this lived moment was very powerful! (Field notes, September 27, 1991)

During the year, Karen's thinking on the value of the support circle shifted, as she felt that grouping the children into smaller support circles would also create another, more personal space for each child to give voice to his or her own stories. Karen talks about this in the following excerpt from our conversation:

> I think what the little support circles have helped me to do is they have helped me to find another avenue for kids to feel heard. . . . I recently. . . read them . . . *All the Secrets of the World* (Yolen, 1991). What it's about is being too young to understand things and I said, "I don't know if you're ever not too young to understand some things cause there's things that even now, I don't understand" and I said, "I want you to think of one of those times." I was able to hit every support circle. . . and Anna of course talked about her parent's divorce and Natalie talked about . . . her uncle's suicide. We got into those incredibly deep, sacred stories you know. And almost all of the kids talked about something that was really close to their heart like that. And then we got into the larger support circle later and the kids were quite willing to share. . . see the safety of

> the little one provided them with the security that, "Yah, it's okay," you know. (Conversation, January 26, 1992)

It has been in this manner that Karen has nurtured a landscape for the children to awaken to and to celebrate their own lived stories. I distinctly remember how I realized that the children were coming to know this story. It occurred one day as Sarah, one of the girls in the classroom, and I were in conversation about how Karen accepts each child as an individual. When I asked Sarah if she had always felt valued and accepted for being the unique person she is, she responded in the following manner:

> Well-l-l-l, hum, not till I got to Karen's class. I always thought I had to be like everybody else, be perfect and stuff. . . . Karen says, "Just be yourself to be perfect. You are perfect in your own way." (Conversation, January 8, 1992)

Similar to the cricket in *I Wish I Were a Butterfly* (Howe, 1987), Sarah knows what the "Old One" meant when he said, "You think I'm beautiful, and so I am" (p. 21). Through listening to the unique, knowing voices of the children with whom she works, Karen has created a space for the children to live a story in which each is "beautiful."

As Karen and the children came together in a community of colearners, they lived in safe relationships in which each unique, knowing voice was encouraged, listened to, and thoughtfully responded to. It has been in this landscape that each has experienced awakenings and transformations in the lived stories. What is important about this community, however, is coming to understand how, at the heart of its foundation, lie two very distinct educative qualities—the celebration of different voices and the learning that occurs when these voices are shared.

PART VI

EDUCATIONAL QUALITIES OF THE LANDSCAPE

CHAPTER 16

Educational Qualities of the Landscape: Desires, Tensions, and Possibilities

F. Michael Connelly and D. Jean Clandinin

In this chapter we turn our attention to the overall educational quality of professional life on the landscape. The epistemological and moral dilemmas created out of teacher movements across the boundary between the classroom and the out-of-classroom places on the landscape have striking consequences for the educational quality of teachers' professional lives.

When we began the four-year study on which this book is based, we thought that the construction of narratives of the professional knowledge landscape would take on a more abstract conceptual quality than it has. We thought that the personalized accounts of teachers' personal practical knowledge that we had been writing up to the beginning of this study would be contextualized by a depersonalized and more sociological and cultural account of teachers' professional knowledge. But, as the stories in these pages show, there is a personal face to professional life on the landscape. It is this personal face that makes it possible to think of the professional knowledge landscape in educational terms.

Craig's (Chapter 14) and Huber and Whelan's (Chapter 15) stories about safe professional places provide a smooth transition to a consideration of the educational quality of professional life on the landscape. Their concern for safety transcends merely professional concerns and reaches into elemental human matters. We want to argue that Craig's and Huber and Whelan's stories, and others in this book, illustrate basic human qualities necessary to having an education. We want to think about professional life as an educational life, not in the sense of this life being part of the profession of education but, rather, that being a professional has educational qualities. Our concern is similar to, but not identical with, Sockett's (1993) interpretation of professionalism as focused on the moral quality of practice. We wish to frame these educational qualities in terms of human desire in order to fix our attention on the underlying human qualities that give rise to professional life and are central to the dilemmas we think the stories in this book so clearly demonstrate.

We discuss three such desires: the desire to tell stories; the desire for relationship; and the desire to think again, to reflect on actions taken and things thought. Everything in the book may be read as testimony to these three desires. Furthermore, to the extent that this reading holds, the gulf between experiencing the professional knowledge landscape as a product of the conduit and experiencing it as a product of these human desires is widened. There may, of course, be something quite fundamentally human—other kinds of desire—that accounts for the philosophy and rhetoric of those who drive the conduit. But our concern is with those who live on the professional knowledge landscape and we view them as working in a place ultimately unfriendly to the human desires we see evident in their professional work.

THE DESIRE TO TELL STORIES OF PRACTICE

In other places, we argued for the use of narrative in educational research on the premise that humans are storytelling creatures who, individually and socially, lead storied lives and tell stories of those lives. The stories in this book are evidence for this view. In page after page we see teachers telling stories. Not only do the teachers tell stories to the researchers but the researchers see and participate in the stories that teachers tell to one another, to children, and to administrators. Furthermore, the chapters are researchers' stories of these stories. We believe that what these pages show goes beyond the unremarkable claim that teachers tell stories. The evidence is that teachers must, of necessity, tell stories. While teachers can be silenced by the sacred theory-practice story in its many guises, stories nevertheless bubble up because they must. It is a way, perhaps the most basic way, that humans make meaning of their experience.

In Chapter 11 we see this bubbling up of the storytelling desire as Janice and Debbie, two beginning teachers, seek each other out in their school. They create times and places—weekends and evenings in the school—to tell stories and, in so doing, to make sense of their practice. Benita also illustrates the storytelling desire as she tells stories of the children and the teachers in the various classrooms in which she served as a substitute teacher. Her stories, told and responded to by Davies and Craig, were central to her inquiry into the image of herself as a good teacher.

While it might be possible to dismiss this desire to tell stories in beginning teachers as an artifact of their insecurity, Hogan's story of her attempt to create professional-development spaces for storytelling belies this interpretation. Pat, an experienced teacher, goes to considerable length to create and maintain a space for her storytelling group. She feels a sense of deep despair at the prospect of losing, and eventual loss of, the space.

These instances, of Janice and Debbie, Benita, Davies and Craig, and Hogan, are striking, almost self-evident expressions of the desire to tell stories. A reading of all of the chapters will show expressions of this storytelling desire.

THE DESIRE FOR RELATIONSHIP

A second, interconnected desire is the desire for relationship. It is interconnected because storytelling is a relational act. Stories are told to others. Furthermore, we believe that there is an inevitability of response that parallels the inevitability of storytelling. Human connections are made between teller and responder. There is a reciprocity in telling and responding that is relational.

This desire for relationship is clearly seen in Chapter 4 when Sonia continues to seek out relationships with other student teachers begun in her third-year teacher education program. This is also seen in Huber's story of herself and Debbie. It would be hard to separate, from a research point of view, the relative force of the desire to tell stories and the desire for relationship that drives these two young teachers together. They need to be together and they need to tell stories. We can follow Janice's desire for relationship when she again establishes a relationship with Karen in Chapter 15. Here, she clearly goes beyond the role of a disinterested researcher. A reader of this chapter clearly senses the personal bond between the two teachers, a bond that transcends ordinary definitions of researcher-participant relationship. Readers may wish to reflect on all of the stories in the book from this point of view. We believe that the kind of narrative inquiry that gave rise to this study of the professional knowledge landscape drew researchers and participants together in the ways that are so vivid in Janice and Karen's relationship. There is a desire for relationship in each of the stories told throughout the book.

Storytellers are influenced by the telling of their own stories. Active construction and telling of a story is educative: The storyteller learns through the act of storytelling. This is why the writing of a story for oneself as audience is an educative act. But our interest here is not in the writing of stories for self but in their telling in relationship. And that, we believe, is doubly educative. It is an education that goes beyond writing for the self because it has a responsive audience, which makes possible both an imagined response and an actual response. These possibilities, the imagining of the response and the response, are important for the storyteller. The possibilities are important in an educative way because the meaning of the story is reshaped and so, too, is the meaning of the world to which the story refers.

THE DESIRE TO THINK AGAIN

The desire to think again is a commonplace in educational studies, made so by John Dewey's (e.g., 1938) work on education and experience. Reflection, thinking again, is a basic human drive for Dewey. One lives, looks backward and forward, and then lives again. It is this desire, more so than the desire to know, that, for Dewey, drove human experience and was the source of education. All of the stories in this book—indeed, the book itself—are stories of thinking again. They are stories of reflection on practice. In Schön's (1992) terms they are stories of reflective practice. We believe that storytelling is a reflective act. Stories are not icons to be learned but inquiries on which further inquiry takes place through their telling and through response to them. In this way, thinking again, relationship, and storytelling are interrelated. Stories of professional practice are stories of relationship and they are stories of thinking again.

For example, in Benita's story seen in Chapters 5, 6, 7, and 9, we see her strong desire to maintain relationships that allowed her to think again about her experiences as a teacher education student and, later, as a teacher. Continuing a relationship with Annie, her cooperating teacher, was desirable because that relationship provided a space for thinking again. When she began teaching and was offered the opportunity to work with Cheryl, she eagerly took it, hoping that she could continue to think again with Cheryl and Annie.

We also see Tim seeking out relationships that would allow him to think again. Even though he worked in a school where narrative and storytelling were not valued on the out-of-classroom part of the landscape, he wrote stories and sought response from his colleagues. It was his desire to think again, interconnected with his desire to tell stories and his desire for relationship, that prompted this move.

These stories of Benita and Tim, and the one of Teresa, have a reflective, think-again quality. Following Dewey the stories are, therefore, educative. They are stories of the educational quality of life on the landscape.

DESIRES IN TENSION WITH THE LANDSCAPE

The out-of-classroom place on the professional knowledge landscape, structured as it is by the sacred theory-practice story, is not a place where the basic human desires, and the reflective relational stories they engender, are nurtured. The stories in this book, time and again, in small, almost unnoticed ways and in large, obvious ways, illustrate this tension between the desires and the nature of the out-of-classroom place on the landscape.

Perhaps the most dramatic story of tension is in the story of Janice and Debbie. Their relationship is completely severed; there is no more storytelling between them; there is no more collaborative thinking. These are all taken away by the unintentional imposition of the sacred theory-practice story by the principal.

But in less dramatic ways, the same tensions, with the same kinds of results in different degree, are seen in other stories. In Tim's story, for example, as the healthy-school story is reinstated in the school, Tim loses the possibility of telling stories and thinking again as the treadmill of out-of-classroom assignments takes hold. Similarly, in Pat's story we see her struggle to change the landscape in ways that will allow her to tell stories, and to think again in relationship. Despite her struggle she loses the opportunity for storytelling and rethinking and is able to stay only in relationships approved by the sacred theory-practice story. In Janice and Karen's story, they are able to maintain a space for the expression of these desires but only by having Janice work with Karen in the classroom. Cheryl, Annie, and Benita manage to create such a space but outside of any particular school's professional knowledge landscape. They create this secret space outside the influence of the sacred theory-practice story. This space is similar to the space Teresa and the researchers created.

THE LANDSCAPE AS EDUCATIVE

We watched new teachers enter the landscape with certain ideas and activities and saw these ideas and activities reshaped in terms of the sacred theory-practice story. We saw experienced teachers try something new that fell into conflict with the sacred story and we saw those activities silenced. The reflective relational stories that are expressions of the three human desires became competing stories that were rapidly redefined on the landscape as conflicting stories. Professionals could live and tell those stories only at their peril. Often they told cover stories. This rendering of these stories may give the sense that we believe that the out-of-classroom place on the landscape is not an educative place for teachers. But this would be a misreading of the view we want to develop. The landscape is clearly educative, but only in a restricted sense.

Teachers on the landscape learn how to act and think in appropriate ways, ways that are sanctioned by others positioned in the conduit. This kind of education is familiar to all. It is the kind of education that occurs when children are taught proper habits, manners, behavior, knowledge, and values. It is the cultivation part of education. Cultivation is what we often hear spoken of as education, that is, when someone acts intentionally on someone else in order to change them, to prepare them for something. For us, this is a process in which someone else blends most fruitfully what is in the environment with what is in the person to be educated. We also understand the process of cultivation as occurring when an individual, a group of individuals, an institution, or a culture acts on a person. Cultivation is one of the main educational processes by which one's moral horizons are constructed. Many of the stories in this book are stories of such cultivation for teachers. They reveal a landscape with a narrow range of what is acceptable.

Cultivation is not the whole of education. If it were, education would be little more than indoctrination. Elsewhere we have written that education involves cultivation, awakenings, and transformations. Cultivation is the living and telling of life stories. But education also involves change in these stories. It involves retelling through awakenings and reliving through transformations. The stories in this book are also stories of awakenings and transformations on the out-of-classroom place on the landscape. We see Janice awakening to the existence of a frame of reference used by her principal, one she finds quite foreign to her way of thinking. While Janice awakens to the possibility of another story, she chooses not to live out a changed story, withdrawing instead to her classroom. We see Tim awakening to the possibility of another professional story he might live and we see him transforming himself into someone who is a leader on the out-of-classroom place on the landscape.

While every cultivation, awakening, and transformation is part of an individual's education, they are not always educative. To use Dewey's (1938) distinction, situations may be miseducative as easily as educative. Ultimately we see most of the cultivations, awakenings, and transformations described in this book as miseducative for teachers. They do not lead to more initiative, increased creativity, more spontaneity, greater reflectivity, or the creation of more moral places in schools. They do not lead to the creation of communally defined moral places. They lead instead to a professional morality defined externally. For example, Pat awakens to the possibilities of telling a new story of professional development. But the transformed living of this new form of professional development is silenced. The awakening is educative because it remains with her as a potential but the educational quality of life on the landscape is not changed. In Janice's story with Debbie, Janice awakens to a form of control in the sacred story that undermines the professional life she is living. In her case the awakening and subsequent transformation are miseducative as her relationship with Debbie is severed and Janice withdraws to her classroom. Something similar happens with Sonia and Josh. While the story may seem quite different, it has the same miseducative plot line. Sonia awakens to the power of the sacred story when she learns that even though Josh is now able to cope with her in the classroom he must be transferred to a special education class. Her relationship with Josh is severed and she, too, withdraws, in silence. Both Janice and Sonia tell these stories as miseducative in terms of learning to live on the landscape. At the conclusion of their stories they feel saddened and powerless.

We also see cultivations, awakenings, and transformations occurring on the in-classroom place on the professional knowledge landscape. Earlier, we noted that classrooms without reflection can be places of endless cultivation. These cultivations occurring without reflection may be miseducative for children—in cases, for example, of gender and culture bias—and they may be noneducative for teachers, who may continue to do things by rote and by habit. Still, the classroom is a place on the landscape where teachers are more able to stay in touch with the human desires outlined in this chapter. There is less intervention by those in the conduit and by the sacred theory-practice story on the in-classroom place on the landscape. It is for this reason that we have called the classroom a safer place for the telling of secret stories. In Chapter 2, in Craig's story of Carla, we see how the conduit, through testing and parent involvement, makes their classroom somewhat unsafe. Still, we see that Craig is able to work with her son and other teachers to tell a story that is clearly an educative one for Carla and for herself. While Craig is clearly living a transformed story of teacher-student relationships, she awakens to the fact that she is not completely in control of this story and that there are risks involved even in the safety of her classroom. In spite of the risks, she continues to live the transformed story. In living the transformed story in her classroom she does create a more moral place in the out-of-classroom place on the landscape in her school. This is seen in the response of other teachers to Carla's education.

PLACES ON THE LANDSCAPE

In this book we have written about two places on the landscape: the in-classroom place and the out-of-classroom place. In Chapter 1 we described the in-classroom place as a relatively safe place for the telling of secret stories, a safe place for the expression of the three human desires. We also described another safe place, one outside the classroom. This place is one in which teachers engage in conversation where stories can be told, reflected back in different ways, retold, and relived in new ways. Throughout this book we found no places on the landscape where this took place. But we did find relationships among people that, for a time, had the quality of a safe place. For example, the research relationship among Annie, Cheryl, and Benita begun in the alternative program and continued through Benita's fourth year of teacher education and her beginning year of teaching has the quality of a safe place. It was a safe place located off the professional knowledge landscape, in the personal landscape defined by the three women. For a time Pat and Stacey and their storytelling group also constituted a safe place on the out-of-classroom place on the professional knowledge landscape. However, this place was, from the beginning, uncertain. In the stories in the book, and more generally in the study on which this book is based, there were no continuing stories of safe places on the out-of-classroom place on the professional knowledge landscape. But such places do exist. As we discussed the work in this book with teachers, they told us stories of their safe places on the professional knowledge landscape. One such telling came from Nancy White, a secondary school teacher. She describes a room in her school where teachers come after class to tell stories in conversation. She wrote:

> I have always felt that our department (myself as head and three other teachers) is a pretty positive place to work. We have absolutely no contact with each other outside of the school and are not social friends, but I think each one of us has a special feeling for what takes place between us during the day.
>
> Our office acts as a bridge between the classroom and the professional knowledge landscape outside of the classrooms. Our office is a place where we tell each other stories about the kids and what we did in the classroom.
>
> It is not unusual for someone to come from a class and say "Boy you should see what I did today" and then tell us. Or to tell stories about particular students (just as often positive as negative)

> or to say "I don't know what to do about . . ." I realize how much we share each other's stories. . . . People freely brag about success and admit failures . . . the environment is very safe and inviting.
>
> But the department is also the bridge between the abstract conduit world and the classrooms. Our conversations allow us to come to terms with what the system expects us to do. For example when the new directives for grade 9 came out, we spent lots of time talking about what we agreed and disagreed with, what we thought was good for kids and where we thought mistakes were being made. In other words we were able to make sense for ourselves of what we were being directed to do. Additionally we were able to change our practice by incorporating parts of the directive. Because we were able to talk and share ideas, we clarified our beliefs and incorporated the directives in a way that was meaningful to us. Even though we were being told we had to move in a particular direction (that we didn't totally agree with) we didn't feel powerless in any way because we had assumed a part in the decision-making process.
>
> When I look at other departments, I can see they don't function as we do—they don't act as a bridge to provide that necessary support for teachers moving from inside to outside the classroom. . . . I know I feel a small tinge of disappointment when I come back to the office after a class and there is no one there. (Nancy White, Reading Log, 1994)

In White's story we see the possibility for safe places on the out-of-classroom place on the landscape. But because it is on the landscape we know that it exists by permission of those positioned in the conduit. We know, as in Pat and Stacey's story, that Nancy's competing story could be seen as conflicting and could be silenced.

We see these safe places as educative places. They are places for the expression of the desires: There is storytelling, there is relationship, there is reflection. As we examine these places it becomes evident that the telling of stories in such places of relationship goes beyond the mere telling of stories to their retelling and reliving. Storytelling can be noneducative, an end in itself, merely a pleasurable activity. But the stories told and retold in these safe places, at least in this study, are educative. They are stories of teachers' learning from their students, of teachers' learning from one another in conversation, of teachers' learning the limits of their own expression on the out-of-classroom place on the professional knowledge landscape.

DESPAIR OR HOPEFULNESS

One reading of this book and of life on the landscape is a reading of despair. Education on the out-of-classroom place on the landscape is, with the exception of a few relatively safe places, an education of conformity directed by people in the conduit and governed by an all-pervasive sacred theory-practice story. In the face of this all-pervasive story, teachers have few choices. In Chapter 1 we noted that teachers could live cover stories. There are examples of these throughout the book. Many teachers on Tim's staff, for example, in the face of the conduit-sanctioned healthy-school story, lived cover stories. These cover stories have something in common with Heilbrun's (1990) more dramatic notion of subversion. We were struck by her comment on Ursula LeGuin.

> But in the introduction to her recent collection of essays, I came on a phrase that further distinguishes us; like so many of her phrases, it reverberates for me: "My goal being always to subvert as much as possible without hurting anybody's feelings." That was always my goal too, but I have not been able to achieve it. I attribute this, not only to the fact that LeGuin may be, and probably is, a nicer person than I, but also to the fact that she is not part of an institution, that she does not find herself always and repeatedly up against a kind of recalcitrance that kindness alone, that wonderful female virtue, cannot penetrate.

But neither cover stories nor LeGuin's subversion are educative ways to live on the landscape. They do not lead to the possibility of retelling and reliving. That is why the reading of professional life provided in this book is, for teachers, so full of despair.

This reading should, however, be a reading of great possibility for those in the conduit. As teachers despair, those in the conduit should rejoice, for the landscape must be a flat, receptive, fertile ground for the cultivation of social initiatives in the form of curriculum programs, value systems, and so on. But the empirical record is quite to the contrary. Since the 1950s, the fields of curriculum implementation and school improvement have mushroomed. They have come into existence because of the failure of the conduit to shape the landscape in ways sanctioned by policymakers and others positioned in the conduit. The main reason given for this ineffectiveness of school reform mandated by those in the conduit is that teachers divert the plans. From the point of view of the conduit, teachers are often seen to be conservative, resistant to reform, and the cultivators of outdated school tradition, whereas those in the conduit are seen to be creating and implementing new and imaginative educational reforms. But teachers, viewed from their position on the landscape, are, in contrast, seen as expressing fundamental human desires and, thereby, rising up to take charge of their moral professional landscape, where they live out their professional lives. What is seen as teacher conservatism and negative resistance from one point of view is seen as the expression of positive educative desires from another.

Where does this leave us? We are left with an irony. Curriculum reformers have a sense of despair about their ability to shape schools. They resort to sophisticated implementation strategies and tactics to minimize teacher influence. Teachers have a sense of despair about their ability to shape their professional landscape. They resort to cover stories and perhaps to subversion to minimize the influence of those in the conduit. Neither force, the reformers in the conduit nor the teachers on the landscape, is satisfied with its sense of effectiveness. Both have a sense of failure about their ability to control and define life on the landscape.

It is in this dual sense of failure that our hope emerges. In the end we do not think it is a tradeoff. The forces for self-definition and for the formation of a moral identity are powerful because they grow out of basic human desires. People tell stories, in relationship and in reflection. They do it because they must. This is what we see bubbling to the surface in the stories in this book. And teachers express human desires in opposition to the imposed moral horizons established by the conduit. This quality of the landscape is central to the hopes we share with everyone concerned with education.

We believe that this book offers hope for both teachers and reformers by naming the qualities of the landscape. We believe that naming the landscape by teachers and by those in the conduit will help compel a rethinking of the ways in which both parties relate to one another. Ultimately, we believe, this will mean a breakdown in the sacred theory-practice story and the creation of new relational stories of theory and practice. These will be stories that acknowledge and validate the educational potential inherent in teachers' reflective, relational storytelling desires. They will also be stories that acknowledge and validate the educational possibilities in the plans for social change formulated by those in the conduit. They will be stories of mutuality between those on the professional knowledge landscape and those outside it. The impositions of the sacred theory-practice story, which are inherently miseducational for those on the landscape and, by implication, for the students in their charge and for the society at large, will, we hope and believe, be replaced by stories that are educational for all. And, should our hope and belief be misplaced, teachers might heed May Sarton's advice "to make myths of our lives" since "It is the only way to live without despair" (1968, p. 39).

References

Barringer, M. D. (1993). How the national board builds professionalism. *Educational Leadership, 50*(60), 18–22.

Base, G. (1986). *Animalia.* Ringwood, Australia: Viking Kestrel.

Belenky, M., Clinchy, B., Goldberger, N., & Tarule, J. (1986). *Women's ways of knowing.* New York: Basic Books.

Cahoon, A. (1991). An address to the Summer Institute of the school district of which Kirkpatrick School is a part.

Carr, D. (1986). *Time, narrative and history.* Bloomington: Indiana University Press.

Carter, K. (1993). The place of story in the study of teaching and teacher education. *Educational Researcher, 22*(1), 5–12, 18.

Clandinin, D. J. (1986). *Classroom practice: Teacher images in action.* Philadelphia: The Falmer Press.

Clandinin, D. J., & Connelly, F. M. (1986). Rhythms in teaching: The narrative study of teachers' personal practical knowledge of classrooms. *Teaching and Teacher Education, 2*(4), 377–387.

Clandinin, D. J., & Connelly, F. M. (1992). The teacher as curriculum maker. In P. W. Jackson (Ed.), *Handbook of research on curriculum: A project of the American Educational Research Association* (pp. 363–401). New York: Macmillan.

Clandinin, D. J., Davies, A., Hogan, P., & Kennard, B. (1993). *Learning to teach, teaching to learn: Stories of collaboration in teacher education.* New York: Teachers College Press.

Clifford, G., & Guthrie, J. (1988). *Ed. school.* Chicago: University of Chicago Press.

Connelly, F. M., & Clandinin, D. J. (1988). *Teachers as curriculum planners: Narratives of experience.* New York: Teachers College Press.

Connelly, F. M., & Clandinin, D. J. (1990). Stories of experience and narrative inquiry. *Educational Researcher, 19*(5), 2–14.

Connelly, F. M., & Clandinin, D. J. (1994). Telling teaching stories. *Teacher Education Quarterly, 21*(1), 145–158.

Craig, C. (1992). *Coming to know in the professional knowledge context: Beginning teachers' experience.* Unpublished doctoral dissertation, University of Alberta, Edmonton.

Craig, C., Dalton, B., & Davies, A. (1992, June). Collaboratively making sense of beginning teaching experience. *Among Teachers,* 5.

Crites, S. (1971). The narrative quality of experience. *Journal of the American Academy of Religion, 39*(3), 291–311.

Cuban, L. (1988). Constancy and change in schools (1880s to the present). In P. W. Jackson (Ed.), *Contributing to educational change: Perspectives on research and practice* (pp. 85–105). Berkeley: McCutchan.

Cuban, L. (1992). Managing dilemmas while building professional communities. *Educational Researcher, 21*(1), 4–11.
Darling-Hammond, L., & Wise, A. E. (1992). Teacher professionalism. In *Encyclopedia of educational research* (pp. 1359–1366). M. C. Alkin (Ed.), New York: Macmillan.
Dewey, J. (1900). *The school and society.* Chicago: University of Chicago Press.
Dewey, J. (1916). *Democracy and education.* New York: Macmillan.
Dewey, J. (1938). *Experience and education.* New York: Collier Books.
Eisner, E. (1988). The primacy of experience and the politics of method. *Educational Researcher, 20,* 15–20.
Elbaz, F. (1983). *Teacher thinking: A study of practical knowledge.* London: Croom Helm.
Fenstermacher, G. D. (1994, in press). The knower and the known in teacher knowledge research. *Review of Research in Education.*
Fullan, M. (1991). *New meaning of educational change.* New York: Teachers College Press.
Goodlad, J. (1990). *Teachers for our nation's schools.* San Francisco: Jossey-Bass.
Graves, D. H. (1983). *Writing: Teachers and children at work.* Portsmouth, NH: Heinemann Educational Books.
Heilbrun, C. G. (1988). *Writing a woman's life.* New York: W. W. Norton & Company.
Heilbrun, C. G. (1990). *Hamlet's mother and other women.* New York: Columbia University Press.
Howe, James. (1987). *I wish I were a butterfly.* (Ed Young, Illus.). San Diego: Harcourt, Brace Jovanovich.
Huberman, M. (1983). Recipes for busy kitchens. *Knowledge: Creation, Diffusion, Utilization, 4,* 478–510.
Johnson, M. (1987). *The body in the mind: The bodily basis of meaning, imagination, and reason.* Chicago: University of Chicago Press.
Johnson, M. (1989). Embodied knowledge. *Curriculum Inquiry, 19*(4), 361–377.
Lampert, M. (1985). How do teachers manage to teach? Perspectives on problems in classrooms. *Harvard Educational Review, 55*(2), 178–194.
Lane, B. C. (1988). *Landscapes of the sacred: Geography and narrative in American spirituality.* New York: Paulist Press.
Lanier, J. E., & Little, J. W. (1986). Research on teacher education. In *Handbook of research on teaching* (pp. 527–569). M. C. Wittrock (Ed.), New York: Macmillan.
Le Guin, U. K. (1989). *Dancing at the edge of the world: Thoughts on words, women, places.* New York: Harper and Row.
Lieberman, A. (1988). *Building a professional culture in schools.* New York: Teachers College Press.
Lieberman, A., & Miller, L. (1992). Professional development of teachers. In M. C. Alkin (Ed.), *Encyclopedia of educational research* (pp. 1045–1051). New York: Macmillan.
Lionni, L. (1967). *Frederick.* New York: Pantheon.
Lyons, N. (1990). Dilemmas of knowing: Ethical and epistemological dimensions

of teachers' work and development. *Harvard Educational Review, 60*(2), 159–180.

MacIntyre, A. (1981). *After virtue: A study in moral theory.* Notre Dame, IN: University of Notre Dame Press.

Marland, P. (1977). *A study of teachers' interactive thoughts.* Unpublished doctoral dissertation, The University of Alberta, Edmonton.

Metzger, D. (1986). Circles of stories. *Parabola, 4*(4).

Mikel Brown, L., & Gilligan, C. (1992). *Meeting at the crossroads: Women's psychology and girls' development.* Cambridge: Harvard University Press.

Noddings, N. (1984). *Caring.* Berkeley: University of California Press.

Oakeshott, M. (1962). *Rationalism in politics.* London and New York: Methuen & Co.

Reddy, M. J. (1979). The conduit metaphor: A case of frame conflict in our language about language. In A. Ortony (Ed.), *Metaphor and thought* (pp.284–324). Cambridge: Cambridge University Press.

Reid, W. A. (1987). Institutions and practices: Professional education reports and the language of reform. *Educational Researcher, 17,* 10–15.

Reynolds, M. C. (Ed.). (1989). *Knowledge base for the beginning teacher.* New York: Pergamon Press.

Russell, T., & Munby, H. (Eds.). (1992). *Teachers and teaching: From classroom to reflection.* London: Falmer Press.

Sarton, M. (1968). *Plant dreaming deep.* New York: Norton.

Schein, E. (1985). *Organizational culture and leadership.* San Francisco: Jossey-Bass.

Schön, D. A. (1983). *The reflective practitioner: How professionals think in action.* New York: Basic Books.

Schön, D. A. (1991). *The reflective turn: Case studies in reflective practice.* New York: Teachers College Press.

Schön, D. A. (1992). A conversation with F. M. Connelly and D. J. Clandinin. *Orbit, 23*(4), 2–5.

Schwab, J. J. (1962). The teaching of science as enquiry. In J. J. Schwab and P. F. Brandwein (Eds.), *The teaching of science.* Cambridge: Harvard University Press.

Schwab, J. J. (1970). *The practical: A language for curriculum.* Washington, DC: National Education Association, Centre for the Study of Instruction. (Reprinted in I. Westbury and N. Wilkoff (Eds.), *Science, curriculum and liberal education: Selected essays.* Chicago: University of Chicago Press, 1978)

Schwab, J. J. (1971). The practical: Arts of eclectic. *School Review, 79*(4), 493–542.

Schwab, J. J. (1973). The practical: Translation into curriculum. *School Review, 81,* 501–522.

Schwab, J. J. (1983). The practical, 4: Something for curriculum professors to do. *Curriculum Inquiry, 13*(3), 239–265.

Shulman, L. S., & Sykes, G. (1986). A national board for teaching? In *Search of a bold standard* (Paper commissioned for the Carnegie Forum on Education and the Economy, Teacher Assessment Project). Stanford, CA: Stanford University, School of Education.

Silverstein, S. (1964). *The giving tree.* New York: Harper and Row.
Sinclair, R. L., & Harrison, A. E. (1988). A partnership for increasing student learning: The Massachusetts Coalition for School Improvement. In K. L. Sirotnik, & J. I. Goodlad (Eds.), *School-university partnerships in action: Concepts, cases, and concerns,* New York: Teachers College Press.
Sockett, H. (1993). *The moral base for teacher professionalism.* New York: Teachers College Press.
Taylor, C. (1989). *Sources of the self: The making of the modern identity.* Cambridge: Harvard University Press.
Tom, A. R., & Valli, L. (1990). Professional knowledge for teachers. In W. R. Houston (Ed.), *Handbook of research on teacher education* (pp. 373–392). New York: Macmillan.
Tyler, R. W. (1950). *Basic principles of curriculum and instruction.* Chicago: University of Chicago Press.
Welker, R. (1992). *The teacher as expert: A theoretical and historical examination.* Albany: State University of New York Press.
Williams, M. (1981). *The velveteen rabbit, or, How toys become real.* Philadelphia: Running Press.
Yolen, J. (1991). *All those secrets of the world.* Boston: Little Brown & Co.

About the Contributors

D. Jean Clandinin is a former teacher, counselor, and school psychologist. She is currently a Professor and Director of the Centre for Research for Teacher Education and Development at the University of Alberta. Working with her colleagues on the ideas in this book has been an exciting experience for her. The conversations on which the book is based have helped her restory her work as a teacher and researcher.

F. Michael Connelly is Professor and Director of the Joint Centre for Teacher Development at the Ontario Institute for Studies in Education (OISE) and the University of Toronto. He is editor of *Curriculum Inquiry* and is the author of several books and many book chapters and articles. He has developed a long-term program of research in the area of research in teacher knowledge. His ongoing collaboration with teachers, administrators, and other colleagues has contributed to his understanding of teacher education and curriculum studies.

Cheryl Craig has been an educator for 18 years. In 1992, she received her Ph.D. from the University of Alberta. Cheryl is currently a Social Sciences and Humanities Research Council of Canada Post-Doctoral Fellow at the Joint Centre for Teacher Development, Ontario Institute for Studies in Education (OISE).

Annie Davies is currently a doctoral student at the University of Alberta, working in the area of teacher education. She has taught for the Calgary Board of Education, at the elementary level for the past 27 years, after receiving her initial teacher-training in Birmingham, England. Annie learns most about teaching by working with children and in collaboration with other teachers. She values her inclusion in research conversations with Jean Clandinin, Pat Hogan, and Cheryl Craig. Such conversations are the catalyst for her writing; they cement friendships that sustain future inquiries.

Ming Fang He was a Master of Arts student in English at Lakehead University from 1989–1991. She received her B.A. in English in the People's

Republic of China, and subsequently taught English in a Chinese university for six years. In 1992 she received her M.Ed. from the Modern Language Center at OISE and began her Ph.D. program in the Joint Centre for Teacher Development at OISE. Her thesis is "The Professional Knowledge Landscapes for Chinese Female Graduates' Enculturation and Acculturation Processes in Canada."

Pat Hogan is currently team-teaching at the grade 1 and 2 level in an inner-city Calgary school. She was formerly a Language Arts Consultant with the Calgary Board of Education and a co-director of the Calgary Writing Project. Pat seeks collaboration in her work with teachers, student teachers, children, and their families. Her imagination is constantly open to "alternative" ways of composing her life as a teacher.

Janice Huber and **Karen Whelan** are currently teaching with Edmonton public schools. As woven into their co-authored chapter in this book, their work together has been based on a strong foundation of faith in one another "as individuals" and it was this common ground which allowed them to honor one another in the collaborative process. Karen and Janice continue to share a safe place in which the authentic stories of their practice are given voice and find meaning. They are thankful that their journey together has become interconnected with the community of people who have also made contributions within this book.

Rosalie Young is a teacher in the Nursing Education Department, Health Sciences Division at George Brown College of Applied Arts and Technology in Toronto, Ontario. She completed her Masters of Education in 1990 and has participated in the Connelly and Clandinin research program on teachers' professional knowledge while continuing her Ph.D. studies at the Joint Centre for Teacher Development at OISE. Rosalie is presently completing her doctoral research in a narrative study of the personal and professional contexts that shape teachers' knowledge development in their professional knowledge landscapes.

Index

Index